"In a broken world, we all experience hurt from our work. But there can be times when pain experienced in the workplace is emotionally devastating. In *When Work Hurts*, Herr is an empathetic guide, helping those who have been wounded at work feel seen and heard. Written from her own experience of pain in the workplace, her journey toward experiencing a renewed sense of calling, and the timeless truth of Scripture, Herr gives gentle and wise prompts to begin the healing process, so we might reclaim a sense of hope in God's purposes for our work."

Matthew Rusten, president of Made to Flourish

"The context of work has been a source of personal fulfillment and joy while also so much disillusionment, pain, and heartache in my life. In this powerful book that weaves together personal anecdotes and theological promises, Meryl Herr points us to a hopeful message that transcends our stories of work hurt without trivializing their impact. For those navigating past or present work hurt as they read this, I hope you will be encouraged—as I was—that our stories are located within a larger narrative that is still unfolding, and our colaboring in stewarding God's creation is not in vain."

Mark Muha, vice president for student development at Biola University

"Whether you're facing a slow burn situation or a sudden change at work, Meryl Herr offers assurance backed by her story and many others. You're not alone, and your pain is real because work hurt cuts deep. She meets you in that hard, honest place—just the person you want across the table when you spill all your soul-searching questions. Pointing to the wisdom of experience and Scripture, she guides you to recover your strength and go forward in ways that are true to who God made you to be."

Rebecca Jantz Johnson, executive leadership coach at Story Solutions

"*When Work Hurts* offers deep insight into the pain and challenges of the workplace, blending personal stories, biblical wisdom, and practical advice. It speaks to those who feel the weight of work hurt, guiding them toward healing and hope through God's redemptive purposes. As a pastor equipping the church for mission in the marketplace, I find this book invaluable. It calls us to face work pain honestly, find resilience, and live as faithful witnesses in our vocations. It is a must-read for anyone seeking to integrate faith and work with purpose and hope."

Artie M. Lindsay Sr., pastor of spiritual formation at Tabernacle Community Church in Grand Rapids, Michigan

"For too many people, work is more of a Genesis 3 rather than Genesis 1 reality. Meryl Herr knows that personally, and she brings honesty and deep compassion to this important book. Packed with stories of work hurt, this highly accessible volume offers at least three beautiful gifts. First, no one who's dealing with disappointments, oppression, confusion, or toxicity at work will feel alone again after reading it. Second, it gives language to help all of us articulate the many ways work goes sideways—which is necessary if the faith-and-work movement is to be grounded in reality, not romanticism. Third, and most important, it plumbs the wisdom of the Bible's historical books to aid contemporary Christians in pursuing everyday faithfulness amid the challenges of the modern workaday world."

Amy L. Sherman, author of *Agents of Flourishing*

"*When Work Hurts* honors sacred places of loss by getting to eye level—gifting us with stories that don't feel preachy or contrived but honest and real. And then, as if hope were a thing that shows up quietly in the dark, it guides readers stepwise into the wisdom and provision of God's story. This book is a simple and profound gem for the many moments when our lives are not."

Jeanette Thomas, cofounder and facilitator of Brandhearted

"*When Work Hurts* is a compassionate, insightful guide for Christians navigating the harsh realities of work life. Meryl Herr—the leading Christian expert on this topic today—masterfully blends empathy, social science, biblical wisdom, and her own experience, offering readers faith-grounded tools to process pain and find healing. This is an important book at an important time. Strongly, emphatically recommended!"

Bryan Dik, author of *Redeeming Work* and coauthor of *Make Your Job a Calling*

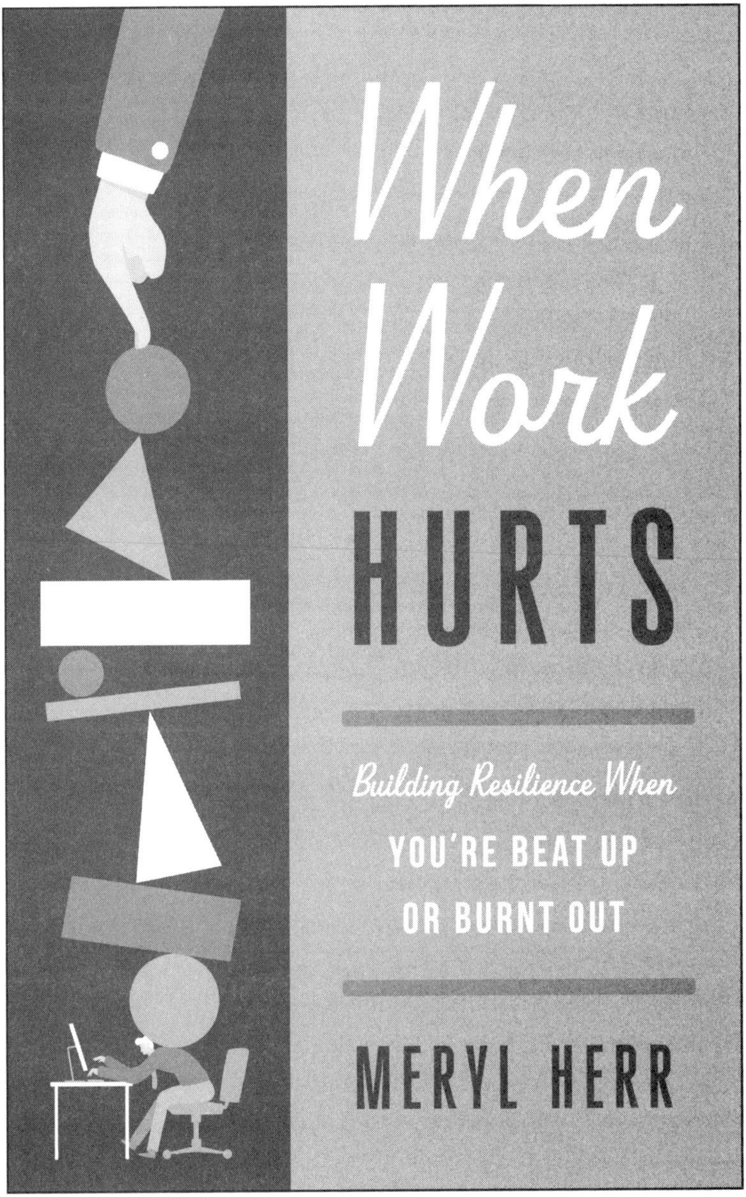

When Work Hurts

Building Resilience When
YOU'RE BEAT UP
OR BURNT OUT

MERYL HERR

An imprint of InterVarsity Press
Downers Grove, Illinois

InterVarsity Press
P.O. Box 1400 | Downers Grove, IL 60515-1426
ivpress.com | email@ivpress.com

©2025 by Meryl Ashley Cantley Herr

All rights reserved. No part of this book may be reproduced in any form without written permission from InterVarsity Press.

InterVarsity Press® is the publishing division of InterVarsity Christian Fellowship/USA®. For more information, visit intervarsity.org.

All Scripture quotations, unless otherwise indicated, are taken from The Holy Bible, New International Version®, NIV®. Copyright © 1973, 1978, 1984, 2011 by Biblica, Inc.™ Used by permission of Zondervan. All rights reserved worldwide. www.zondervan.com. The "NIV" and "New International Version" are trademarks registered in the United States Patent and Trademark Office by Biblica, Inc.™

Published in association with the literary agency of WordServe Literary Group Ltd., www.wordserveliterary.com.

While any stories in this book are true, some names and identifying information may have been changed to protect the privacy of individuals.

"The Valley of Vision" by Arthur Bennett is used with permission from The Banner of Truth Trust, Edinburgh, UK.

The publisher cannot verify the accuracy or functionality of website URLs used in this book beyond the date of publication.

Cover design: Faceout Studio
Interior design: Jeanna Wiggins
Images: ©Yellow_Man/Shutterstock.com

ISBN 978-1-5140-1024-2 (print) | ISBN 978-1-5140-1025-9 (digital)

Printed in the United States of America ∞

Library of Congress Cataloging-in-Publication Data
Names: Herr, Meryl, 1980- author.
Title: When work hurts : building resilience when you're beat up or burnt out / Meryl Herr.
Description: Downers Grove, Illinois : IVP, [2025] | Includes bibliographical references.
Identifiers: LCCN 2024038350 (print) | LCCN 2024038351 (ebook) | ISBN 9781514010242 (paperback) | ISBN 9781514010259 (ebook)
Subjects: LCSH: Work–Religious aspects–Christianity. | Burn out (Psychology)–Religious aspects–Christianity.
Classification: LCC BT738.5 .H47 2025 (print) | LCC BT738.5 (ebook) | DDC 248.8/8–dc23/eng/20241102
LC record available at https://lccn.loc.gov/2024038350
LC ebook record available at https://lccn.loc.gov/2024038351

In loving memory of

Miss Dale Quin

who taught me to love words

Contents

INTRODUCTION: The Pain of Work — 1

1. When the Walls Fall Down — 15
2. Feeling like an Exile — 31
3. Learning to See in the Dark — 51
4. Sensing a New Calling — 67
5. Staying on Task — 86
6. Making Sense of It All — 100
7. Working in a Battle Zone — 116
8. Being Exploited and Oppressed — 132
9. Realizing It's Me — 149
10. Remembering to Hope — 162
11. Working in the New Jerusalem — 174

ACKNOWLEDGMENTS — 183

NOTES — 185

INTRODUCTION

The Pain of Work

I DON'T KNOW HOW LONG I lay on the floor sobbing. Maybe it was five minutes. Maybe it was fifty. Time stood still the second I uttered, *I lost my job.*

That was August 2010. I can still remember the feel of the tear-stained carpet against my face. Since May 2009, when my full-time job as a pastoral resident had ended, I had bounced between unemployed and underemployed. But in the summer of 2010, I landed a job developing middle school math curriculum. It was a limited-term, contract position, but it was going to compensate me enough to pay for the PhD program I was starting that fall.

It was a remote job. Still, the company brought all of the curriculum developers to their headquarters for two days of training. It felt amazing to be part of a team and to have work that used my skills and paid well. A month into the job, the project supervisor called me for a quick performance review. They loved my work. I loved doing the work. It seemed like a win-win. But the next day he called again. It caught me by surprise since I'd just talked to him. It could only mean more good news, right? Wrong. So so so so wrong.

I can't recall the entire conversation. But I remember the essence of it. *Meryl, we just had some budget meetings, and we have to make some cuts. We're eliminating your position.*

I couldn't make sense of it. Wasn't my work amazing? Why did my position get eliminated? Why not one of the other curriculum developers? Why me? In an instant, my job disappeared. I picked up my phone and called my husband. I told him I had lost my job. And then I collapsed to the floor and wept. I was devastated.

FULL OF HOPES AND DREAMS

Once upon a time, I felt excited about work. I had a vague sense of calling—that God was inviting me to help people develop deeper relationships with him. That calling gave me enough direction to go to seminary. When I graduated with my Master of Divinity degree, I felt this Holy Spirit current charging in my veins and a deep assurance that my friends and I had been well-equipped to steward the gospel no matter where God sent us. That passion stayed alive through two years of a pastoral residency. And then the residency ended. In the middle of the Great Recession.

At that time, churches were laying off more pastors than they were hiring. My husband had also been a pastoral resident. We thought the odds of finding one ministry position were better than the odds of finding two. For a few months, I worked retail while my husband temped and looked for a new job. When my boss asked for my availability, I told her I could work anytime other than Sunday mornings. But she would never schedule me for more than twenty-nine hours per week. I wasn't looking for the benefits that came with being full-time. I simply wanted to work as much as I could to earn money. I scrambled for other gigs to try to supplement our income.

When my husband got a new job, we moved. And no one in the new town would hire me—at least, no one in the types of jobs I was seeking, ones that used my gifts and my training. I sent out résumé after résumé. I even went to a temp agency. I got a little worried when the staffing associate, Rose, asked me if I considered myself to be a professional. I was the only prospective employee in business dress. She found me a job making cold calls for a local veteran's affairs organization. I lasted two days.

At my lowest point in all of this, my husband would come home from work for lunch and find me in my sweats, eating lunch, and watching *The Jerry Springer Show*, the trashy talk show that came on after the WGN midday news. The show took up topics like contentious love triangles, revenge plots, and paternity test revelations. Somehow the show brought consolation. I would think, "At least my life's not that bad."

Around that time, I started having conversations with a few trusted mentors who encouraged me to get a doctorate. I liked the idea, but I needed a job to pay for it. That curriculum writing job was perfect. It was a ten-month contract developing pre-algebra and algebra curriculum. (I realize this might sound like a lot of people's worst nightmare, but I'm a total math nerd. I majored in math, and I was even on my school's math team from seventh through twelfth grade. Feel free to laugh. We were national champs three out of four years I was in high school, and it gave me lots of opportunities for travel and to experience how easily I can crack under pressure.)

Anyway, I was fine capitalizing on my love for math to pay for my PhD in not-math. It felt like the Lord's provision. The job would be part-time and it would pay about forty thousand dollars—slightly under what I needed for tuition. Truly a miracle. Until it wasn't. Until that work got yanked out from under me. Until I discovered that salty carpet is equal parts scratchy and disgusting—but also, oddly grounding when work has leveled you.

WORK HAS HURT MANY OF US

What I wish I had known then was that I wasn't alone.

I lost my job as the United States began climbing out of the Great Recession. That was a time of severe global economic decline from 2007 to 2009 that stemmed largely from two related crises: the burst of the housing bubble and the financial meltdown of big banks. Millions of people around the world lost their jobs. The unemployment rate in the United States rose sharply, from 5 to 10 percent, indicating that millions of people were looking for work and not able to find it.[1]

That wouldn't be the last time a massive employment crisis would sweep the globe. When the coronavirus pandemic hit in 2020, roughly 250 million full-time jobs were lost around the world—four times the amount of jobs lost during the Great Recession.[2] In the United States, over 20 million people lost their jobs at the start of the pandemic.[3] As people returned to work and the economy tried to rebound, a new phenomenon emerged—the Great Resignation. Between June 2021 and December 2022, over 4 million people *per month* quit their jobs.[4] Prior to the pandemic, an average of 1.8 million people per month were laid off or terminated from their jobs, and since the pandemic, the number has gone down slightly to about 1.5 million people per month.[5] Still, that's a lot of job loss.

Those statistics are jaw-dropping, yet they don't even begin to account for all of the other disappointment and disillusionment that happen at work—the frustration and sometimes outright abuse we endure: not getting the interview, job, or promotion we wanted; being the victim of bullying, discrimination, or harassment; holding out for even a standard-of-living raise; wishing our boss wasn't such a tyrant; or wanting our coworkers to treat us with dignity. The list could go on and on. And it does.

Let's start with burnout. In a 2022 survey of employees from fifteen countries, McKinsey & Company found that approximately one in four employees were experiencing burnout.[6] Both Gallup and Deloitte report that at least three out of four of those working in the United States have experienced burnout sometime at work.[7] In 2024, approximately one out of every four employees in the United States very often or always felt burned out at work.[8]

What contributes to the burnout? Gallup says the main reasons are "unfair treatment at work, unmanageable workload, unclear communication from managers, lack of manager support, and unreasonable time pressure."⁹ (Those of us who have experienced burnout probably don't need a survey to tell us this.) When the folks at Gallup looked at burnout rates across industries in the United States, K-12 teachers had the highest rate at 44 percent. But nearly a third of people working in law, health care, retail, government or public policy, professional services, and college or university jobs were also burned out.[10]

And then there's the harassment and discrimination. One in five employees globally have experienced at least one form of violence or harassment at work.[11] Within the United States, 38 percent of women and 14 percent of men report having been sexually harassed in the workplace or at school.[12] The American Association of Retired Persons (AARP) found that two in three workers in the United States who are ages forty-five and over have experienced discrimination at work due to their age.[13] In 2020, Gallup found that 24 percent of Black employees and 24 percent of Hispanic employees had experienced racism at work in the previous year.

Work engagement is another indicator of what is and is not working well at work. It's a measure of an employee's enthusiasm for and involvement in their daily work. It's probably not surprising that only one in four workers globally and one in three workers in the United States are actually engaged in their jobs.[14] Writing about the current state of work in capitalist societies, Sarah Jaffe says that we live in an era in which we're supposed to love our jobs, but most of us don't. Jaffe writes, "The new work ethic, in which work is expected to give us something like self-actualization,

> *Most jobs will not make us happy, and even the ones that do will often be a source of deep frustration.*
>
> **SARAH JAFFE**

cannot help but fail. Most jobs will not make us happy, and even the ones that do will often be a source of deep frustration."[15] Ugh!

THE GAP BETWEEN GOD'S DESIGN FOR WORK AND WHAT WE EXPERIENCE

This isn't the way it's supposed to be. Work isn't supposed to be fraught with so much disappointment and despair. God designed work to be a delight. In fact, God works. In six days, God formed and filled our world, creating us, his image bearers on the last day (Genesis 1). And God continues to work, caring for all that he has made.

God saw the completed creation and called it very good (Genesis 1:31). He delighted in the work of his hands. And I believe that's what he intended for us to experience in our work. But sin destroyed that hope. After Adam and Eve disobeyed God by eating the forbidden fruit, God punished them and cursed the ground—both of which had dire consequences for our work.

> To the woman he said,
> "I will make your pains in childbearing very severe;
>   with painful labor you will give birth to children.
> Your desire will be for your husband,
>   and he will rule over you."
>
> To Adam he said, "Because you listened to your wife and
>   ate fruit from the tree about which I commanded you,
>   'You must not eat from it,'
>
> "Cursed is the ground because of you;
>   through painful toil you will eat food from it
>   all the days of your life.
> It will produce thorns and thistles for you,
>   and you will eat the plants of the field.
> By the sweat of your brow
>   you will eat your food
> until you return to the ground,

since from it you were taken;
for dust you are
and to dust you will return." (Genesis 3:16-19)

When we read the phrases "painful labor" and "painful toil" in Genesis 3:16-17, we likely think about physical pain. Painful labor. Yes, it is, with and without an epidural. Painful toil. Obviously. Splinters and sore muscles seem like the logical outcome of working the ground. But the Hebrew word translated as "painful" can also mean causing "mental and emotional suffering."[16] This word shows up in one other place in Scripture. In Genesis 5:29 we read of Noah's birth: "He [Lamech] named him Noah and said, 'He will comfort us in the labor and painful toil of our hands caused by the ground the LORD has cursed.'" For generations after the fall, people experienced such anguish in their work that they needed comfort and relief. Many of us have the same need today. Work can certainly break our bodies. But more often it breaks our hearts.

Even when we know work will not be easy, we go into it with high hopes. We'll get along fabulously with our boss and coworkers. Our performance reviews will be glowing. And we'll stay in the job long enough to make a real impact. Those high expectations can make the disappointment, disillusionment, and devastation we experience in our work all the more jarring. Realizing the enormous gap between expectations and reality causes immense frustration and heartache. When work doesn't go the way we hope or the way it ought, the anger, grief, and shame we experience can be profound, and no amount of Ben and Jerry's can fix it. Eating our feelings can't pick us up and put us back together.

> *Work can certainly break our bodies. But more often it breaks our hearts.*

DEALING WITH OUR WORK HURT

When work beats us up, burns us out, or breaks our hearts, giving up and staying down on the floor can seem like viable options. We could wallow in our sadness. We could ignore our pain or try to numb it as we try to move on to the next project or next job. But here's the problem with both those options: they make our light grow dim. Brené Brown warns about the consequences of numbing our pain: "We *cannot* selectively numb emotion," she writes. "If we numb the dark, we numb the light. If we take the edge off pain and discomfort, we are, by default, taking the edge off joy, love, belonging, and the other emotions that give meaning to our lives."[17]

Since he brought them out of Egypt, God has intended for his people to be a light to the nations (cf. Deuteronomy 4:5-8; Isaiah 42:6). Jesus told his followers,

> You are the light of the world. A town built on a hill cannot be hidden. Neither do people light a lamp and put it under a bowl. Instead they put it on its stand, and it gives light to everyone in the house. In the same way, let your light shine before others, that they may see your good deeds and glorify your Father in heaven. (Matthew 5:14-16)

Jesus calls us to let our light shine brightly—and we do so by doing good work and, in that, pointing others to him. As Steve Garber puts it, our work is integral to the mission of God regardless of whether we work as a pastor or plumber, missionary or math teacher.[18] But the disappointment, disillusionment, and devastation we experience in our work can dim our light. Heck, work-related hurt can make us want to crawl under a bush and hide. Ignoring our hurt can dim our light, but—worse—it can also cause us to spread darkness. Richard Rohr put it this way:

> If we cannot find a way to make our wounds into sacred wounds, we invariably become cynical, negative, or bitter.

This is the storyline of many of the greatest novels, myths, and stories of every culture. If we do not transform our pain, we will most assuredly transmit it—usually to those closest to us: our family, our neighbors, our co-workers, and, invariably, the most vulnerable, our children.[19]

We have to tend to our pain. If we don't deal with our work hurt, eventually it will deal with us.

When work hurts us—physically or emotionally—it's as if a violent wind rattles our flame and threatens to snuff us out. When reduced to a flicker, we no longer burn brightly. Jesus calls us to be beacons of hope. I imagine his followers as millions of tiny lighthouses illuminating the way to him in the midst of life's challenges. If we don't attend to the pain that work causes, we'll fade into the shadows, turn inward, and wonder what we could have done to keep the light on.

LEARNING TO BE RESILIENT

Resilience is "the capacity of a system to withstand or recover from significant challenges."[20] It's the ability to flicker from time to time without going out. It's also the ability to burn brightly again after nearly being extinguished. Keeping the candle burning pushes back the darkness in this world. It sustains us, and it helps other people see the radiance of Christ—the light that God has shined in our hearts (2 Corinthians 4:6).

My suspicion is that very few of us have received formal training on how to be resilient in our work. I never took When Work Hurts 101. In school, I gained the technical and relational skills to get a job, do it well, and build a career. No one intentionally prepared me for the hard days, the harsh words, and the heavy burdens that can come with our work. Even the workplace training I have received has fallen woefully short. Our training videos may teach us how to recognize workplace bullying or report sexual harassment, but they don't equip us to grieve, process, and recover from it.

Much of the training I have received has come through the proverbial "school of hard knocks." The same is true for many. We've learned to be resilient through experience. We've had to endure frustrating, stressful, or grueling work because we didn't have any other viable options. I've also learned about resilience by watching others endure their own battles with work hurt. Both of my parents started their own businesses when I was young. I recall the stress it caused them. My mom eventually had to close her company. She got laid off from another job while I was in college, and for years she worked for someone she described as "the worst boss anyone could imagine." But my parents never gave up. They kept going.

I've also learned something about resilience by studying the Scriptures and observing God's people in some of their most difficult moments. In particular, I think about the time when the people of Judah found themselves sitting in a pile of rubble, utterly destroyed by something many of them never expected would happen in their lifetime. They watched their beloved city of Jerusalem sieged and then burned to the ground. And then most of them were carried off into exile.

Over the course of this book, we're going to walk through the story of the Israelites from the fall of Jerusalem, their journey into exile, and back home again. No single book of the Bible covers that time period. To get the full story, we're going to dip our toes into several books and go for a long swim in another. Second Chronicles, the Psalms, Isaiah, Jeremiah, and Lamentations will give us some of the historical context. We'll also take a quick look at Daniel, Haggai, and Zechariah. But we'll spend the majority of our time in what the Hebrew Scriptures treated as a single book: Ezra-Nehemiah. They describe the journey home and the rebuilding, renewing, and restoring work that happened among a people who had once been sitting in the rubble.

I hope you'll discover that we can find solidarity in their story because they experienced nearly catastrophic grief. Yet they kept going. With God's help, they kept the light on and remained faithful to God's call not only to pick up the pieces but also to engage a broken world. And they did that even in the face of more challenges, opposition, and heartbreak.

If God's people could be resilient then, in those circumstances, we can learn to be resilient now, in ours. That's where we're going to start—with our circumstances. We're going to unpack some of the ways work can level us. We'll talk about what it looks and feels like when work beats us up, burns us out, or breaks our hearts. I'll introduce you to several people who have experienced all types of work hurt. They courageously and generously shared their stories because of their desire to help you. In most cases, I've changed names and details to protect their identities.

> *With God's help, the Israelites kept the light on and remained faithful to God's call not only to pick up the pieces but also to engage a broken world.*

I'll share more of my story as well. When I lost my job in 2010, I never imagined that other people's work would become central to my work. For over a decade, I've studied work—from how college students choose certain careers to what university administrators think about their jobs. I've interviewed people who have experienced so much organizational dysfunction and trauma that they've cried when telling me about it. I've spoken with people whose toxic work environments have filled them with fear. And I've walked alongside friends and students who have been treated poorly at work and who have lost their jobs or their businesses. I've learned that work can bring tremendous joy but often brings incredible sorrow. I can't help but groan.

I want better for these people; I want better for all of us. But there's no easy fix. The causes of work hurt are legion. Some of them are systemic. Through my work at the Max De Pree Center for Leadership at Fuller Seminary, I help equip organizational leaders who can catalyze change and promote the flourishing of their employees. Change takes time, though. So while we yearn for more organizations to have healthy cultures and prioritize the well-being of their people, we can learn to be more resilient in our everyday work. And if you're an organizational leader or a manager, I hope that this book will give you a new perspective on how people experience their work so that you'll be inspired to make work better.

We'll also turn our attention to the story of the Israelites to see how they responded when the Babylonians leveled them. We'll discover the practices they used to stoke the fire in their hearts so that it wouldn't go out. And we'll learn what it takes to keep the light on. Because we, my friends, are the light of the world. It's hard to be a city on a hill when we're a smoldering pile of rubble. As we heal from our work-related hurt and develop resilience to deal with it again and again, we can better respond to the call that God has for us to be rebuilders, renewers, repairers, and restorers as we partner in his redemptive work in the world.

WORK HURT CLINIC

When we're in severe pain, whether from a sore throat or broken ankle, we need help to get well. If we can, we go to the nearest clinic where a medical professional asks us about our symptoms, assesses our pain, makes a diagnosis, and prescribes a treatment plan. I'm a doctor, but of philosophy, not medicine. I can't diagnose your condition or prescribe a course of treatment, but I can offer some prompts and suggestions for you to reflect on your work hurt and pursue healing. At the end of each chapter, you'll find a Work Hurt Clinic where you can revisit some of the main ideas and begin to apply some of the practices.

Symptoms: In your work, have you now or in the past experienced any of the following?

- ▶ Grief
- ▶ Anger
- ▶ Burnout
- ▶ Frustration
- ▶ Heartbreak
- ▶ Disappointment
- ▶ Emotional numbing

Causes: To what extent did you identify with the work hurt examples included in this chapter?

- Job loss
- Underemployment
- Unemployment
- Frustrating job search
- Bullying
- Discrimination
- Harassment
- Low or inequitable pay
- Toxic boss
- Burnout

Pain:

- On a scale of 1 (minimal pain) to 10 (severe pain), how would you rate the pain that your work hurt has caused?
- Do you have pain from work hurt that you've neglected or numbed?
- To what extent might your pain be affecting your current work, relationships, or well-being?

Care: Continue reading this book and consider discussing your work hurt with a friend.

When the Walls Fall Down

AFTER TEN YEARS IN educational and nonprofit leadership in her community of Athens, Georgia, Lora had a vision for what could help children flourish—schools that were student-centered and creative. The events of 2020 helped her refine that vision. As racial tensions rose in the United States and she began receiving invitations to speak on race-related issues, Lora started to reflect on her educational journey as a Black child who attended a predominately White private school. She lamented not having Black cultural spaces to explore that part of her identity while growing up. That's what Athens needed—a school that would focus on the thriving of the community's Black youth. The idea came like a torrent, she told me. The call to start Joy Village School was unmistakable.

Joy Village School welcomed twenty-five students in the fall of 2022. Drawing on the West African tradition of Harambe, students began their days with chants, cheers, and affirmations before attending to their core subjects of math, language arts, and Black history. After a focused reading time, they participated in enrichment activities such as drumming, chess, coding, cooking, basketball, and step. Everything seemed to be flourishing, except Lora was crumbling on the inside.

Running a school required leasing a building and paying staff—two huge expenses. Lora took out personal loans to help cover the costs, and she began to focus thirty to forty hours per week on fundraising on top of her teaching and administrative responsibilities. She took any opportunity she had to talk to people about the school and ask for a donation. She made pleas via social media, telling the world, "We're having such a joyful experience here." But what Lora felt was the antithesis of joy. She told me,

> I set out to create this school and do work that was meaningful to me, but the job I ended up doing was 20 percent of the meaningful, lifegiving work. I spent 80 percent of my time fundraising and writing grants—thirty grants that year, and I was out at community events all the time meeting people and trying to raise money.

She admitted, "I was maintaining a façade of togetherness when on the inside I was drowning a lot of the time."

Lora was exhausted. She was working seventy to eighty hours per week. At one point she contracted Covid-19 and shingles, but she didn't take time off. She had to keep the school afloat. Still, she put a happy face on even though she and her school were crumbling. Lora was drowning in debt and eventually had to declare personal bankruptcy. When the school finally closed at the end of its first year, it felt like a mercy while at the same time sending Lora spiraling deep into a midlife crisis. Lora's dream died, and with the closing of Joy Village School came a flood of grief.

The pain we experience in our work can vary in severity and scope. Researchers believe the brain processes socio-emotional pain the same way it processes pain from a physical injury.[1] Like the pain we feel in our body, the emotional pain we experience from work can be chronic or acute. It can be tolerable or debilitating. It can dissipate or accumulate. Regardless, it hurts and cries out for our attention.

WHEN WORK DISAPPOINTS

Disappointment at work is an everyday experience for most of us. It happens when work fails to live up to our hopes or expectations. We don't finish everything on our to-do list. Only one person attends the online event we planned. Customers prefer our competitor's product to ours. Our boss tells us that our report needs another round of revisions. We overcook the chicken—again.

It's all frustrating. But for the most part, we can deal with that level of disappointment. We reexamine our priorities and brush up our time management strategies. We receive the one attendee with hospitality and gratitude and think about how we might better promote the next event. We do some market analysis to reassess our customers' needs. We dig in and fix the report. We finally buy a new oven.

But sometimes the disappointments are more profound. I think of a 2019 Indeed commercial that depicts a group of professionals standing in a conference room.[2] At the front of the room, we see Claire, gleaming in expectation as her boss prepares to announce the name of the company's newest vice president. As soon as the "m" sound rolls off her boss's tongue, Claire's face begins to fall. The promotion went to her colleague Michael. We get the sense that she had been passed over before. She's crushed.

In 2022, news outlets began talking about the "Great Resignation" because people in the United States were quitting their jobs in record numbers.[3] They quit their jobs during the Great Resignation because work had become a Great Disappointment. The Pew Research Center found that people who quit their jobs during that period tended to do so because of low pay, no opportunities for advancement, and feeling disrespected at work.[4] Patrick quit a job for all three of those reasons.

He was working as an adjunct professor for a small college. From the outset, the pay was terrible. Patrick had dreamed of becoming a professor for years and thought he could tolerate the low pay for a season in exchange for an opportunity to get his foot in the door. At one point, he did the math and figured he could have been making about the same amount working retail. That was rather infuriating since the teaching job required a doctorate; still, he was willing to accept it for a while.

But soon, the possibilities for advancement went from slim to nil. He felt like some people in the university didn't respect him. Others made him feel like he had nothing to contribute to the school beyond the few tasks they had asked him to do. Patrick's disappointment became so profound that it festered into resentment and bitterness. Like a poison, it started seeping into his relationships and his work. Even his students began to pick up on his cynicism. He knew he should quit but needed the money and wanted to hold out hope that it would get better. But it didn't. Things got worse. And he left. To Patrick, it felt like a bad breakup, like waking up to the realization of unrequited love. And it hurt.

WHEN WORK DISILLUSIONS US

Disappointment leads to pain; but the *disillusionment* we experience at work can also hurt us. Disillusionment comes when work challenges some of our deeply held assumptions.

My husband and I got married in 2005 while we were both in seminary, but we knew that we couldn't afford for both of us to be in school at the same time. So we agreed that one would work full-time while the other finished their degree, and then we would switch. That's how I came to teach middle school math. Two months after we got married, I landed the job at a local Christian school.

I was so excited about the job because I loved teaching math, and I was eager to help my students understand how math fit into God's big story. I decorated my classroom, designed some fun learning activities, and developed relationships with the other teachers. I knew the job would be difficult—four different math classes and three electives to prep and almost no support from our special education staff. But no one prepared for me for the biggest challenge I would face: the parents.

I would get an earful from parents when their students had to sit the bench at a basketball game because they weren't passing pre-algebra. It didn't matter that I offered to help their students before school, after school, and during study hall. It didn't matter that I had extra credit work available for all students. To these parents, the fact that their kids weren't passing was my fault and mine alone.

Another parent was so hostile toward me that the principal would no longer let her communicate with me on the phone or in person without an administrator present. It turned out that this mom had a rather tumultuous home life and opted to take it out on me. I decided I would take her verbal abuse again in a heartbeat if it kept her from unleashing her anger on her son, who was my student.

And then there were the parents of eighth graders who pressured me to recommend their children for the best math classes at their new high schools, even when I knew the student had little chance of success. If I declined, I was "ruining their lives." That math placement would affect their ability to get into Harvard. I secretly wished I could tell one mom, "Ma'am, right now your daughter appears to be more interested in boys and basketball than equations and inequalities. Maybe let's work together to help her learn to solve for x so that she passes my class and doesn't have to repeat pre-algebra as a freshman."

Over time, the parents' persistent enmity wore me down. I had no idea that people who paid money to send their children to a Christian school could be so mean. The way they treated me jilted me out of my naiveté. Note to my twenty-five-year-old self: not everyone in a Christian school community will act Christlike.

Disillusionment at work is no respecter of persons. Catherine was a young mom who had taken a new job to support herself and her kids. She was quite good at her job, and her boss noticed. He gave her more responsibility. And then he gave her something she didn't want—sexual harassment. He hit on her. In an instant, any illusions Catherine had about her boss's professionalism shattered. She quit immediately. But the hurt persisted. She had liked her work. She had needed the income the job provided. And her boss's transgression siphoned away any sense of joy and delight she felt in it.

WHEN WORK DEVASTATES US

Devastate: "to reduce to chaos, disorder, or helplessness: overwhelm."[5] The word that particularly captures my attention there is "reduce." Work can make us feel small. It can bring us to our knees, to the floor. Has work ever made you feel this way before? That's what happened to Rachel.

I interviewed her two weeks after she was laid off. Rachel worked for a large, regional bank in the United States. Throughout her twenty-year tenure with the bank, Rachel had several roles in both local branches and regional management. In the fall of 2023, the company mentioned that it would be making some budget cuts. Hers wasn't the only bank making cuts: several multinational and global banks laid off thousands of employees that year.[6] The first round of layoffs happened in November. She survived those but knew that more could be coming in the new year. Realistic in her outlook, she knew she could be laid off. Still, she didn't let that deter her from focusing on her job.

At 8:30 a.m. on a Wednesday, Rachel received an email from her manager asking to join her for a check-in via video chat at 9:00 a.m. The request felt odd and out of character. She texted her husband, "I think I'm about to lose my job." When her boss began the conversation with small talk, Rachel knew. Her boss told her that her work was done at that moment. Rachel told me, "My whole world just crashed."

Job loss is incredibly painful, and it's an all-too-common occurrence today. It's also far from the only form of devastation we can experience in work. Even when our position isn't on the chopping block, there are thousands of different ways we can have our hearts broken on the job. I think about those whose bosses never encourage and only ever tear them down. Or those whose colleagues take the credit for their ideas. And then there are those who witness violence, physical harm, and even death in the workplace. It's too much. Come, Lord Jesus.

> Even when our position isn't on the chopping block, there are thousands of different ways we can have our hearts broken on the job.

When work wounds us, sometimes it leaves little cracks—cracks small enough that we can mend with patience, time, and care. Other times work smashes us to pieces. When that happens, we can stay on the tear-stained carpet for a while. But even though it feels safer on the floor, where there's no way we can fall any further, we can't live there. Eventually we need to get up and survey the damage.

The Bible offers some insight on how to stand up and examine all the broken pieces in and around us after work demolishes us. There's a place in the Bible where we see God's people leveled, their city reduced to rubble. And there's a man who finds himself left to take in all the destruction. Maybe if we study his response, we can glean some wisdom for what to do when work tears us apart.

A BEAUTIFUL CITY, BROKEN

Jerusalem was a remarkable city. But it wasn't always that way. Before it became the geographical and spiritual center of Israel's life, Jerusalem was a Jebusite fortress in the hill country of Judah, the southernmost of the twelve tribes of Israel. The Jebusites were one of the Canaanite tribes that God's people were supposed to drive out of the Promised Land but didn't. *The Baker Encyclopedia of the Bible* describes Jebusite Jerusalem this way: "Occupied by the Jebusites, it was a pocket of neutral territory between the northern and southern sections of David's united kingdom and politically acceptable to both."[7] Scholars believe Jebusite Jerusalem was home to about one thousand people.[8]

Shortly after David became king, he and his men marched on Jerusalem and conquered it. The Bible tells us, "David then took up residence in the fortress and called it the City of David. He built up the area around it, from the terraces inward" (2 Samuel 5:9). David unified the tribes into one nation, and Jerusalem became its political and religious center.

David wanted to continue building. He wanted to build a temple to house the ark of God's covenant that he and his men had reclaimed from the Philistines. But God told him that the task of building the temple would fall to someone else. That someone else was David's son Solomon. Solomon oversaw much of Jerusalem's development. It's believed that Jerusalem's population grew to between four and five thousand during his reign.[9] God chose Solomon to build the temple. It was a massive undertaking that took seven years to complete (1 Kings 6:38).

First, Solomon chose Mount Zion as the site for the temple. For the Israelites, the temple would come to symbolize the place where heaven and earth met, and it was the place where God dwelled among his people. Second, Solomon spared no expense on its construction. He paid the King of Tyre for the best lumber from Lebanon. Solomon used the cedar, cypress, and high-quality stone to construct and decorate the temple. The inside of the temple had intricate carvings (1 Kings 6:18). The inner sanctuary and its altar were covered in pure gold (1 Kings 6:20-22). The furnishings were just as ornate (1 Kings 7:13-51). The temple was lavish. And its extravagance pointed to the holiness of God. One scholar described the temple this way,

"Solomon's temple was the embodiment of Israel's religious and national identity. Its setting and design manifested Yahweh's presence, while its splendor provided tangible evidence of his favor."[10]

After the work had been completed, God consecrated the temple and promised to establish Solomon's throne if he would follow the Lord "faithfully with integrity of heart and uprightness" (1 Kings 9:4). But the Lord added a condition. If Solomon and his people chose not to follow God, he would reject his people and the temple would "become a heap of rubble" (1 Kings 9:8).

Fast forward about 360 years. David's kingdom has been split in two—Israel to the north and Judah to the south. Israel has been raided by the Assyrians and many of its inhabitants have been taken into captivity. And now Jerusalem, the capital of Judah—including the temple, which was the center of Israel's religious life and the symbol of God's presence among them—is indeed a heap of rubble.

Sadly in our modern times we don't have to look far to see cities reduced to ruin and rubble. When Russia invaded Ukraine in 2022, entire cities were demolished, their buildings blown to smithereens. Many residents of Kyiv gathered a few precious belongings and took shelter in subway tunnels while bombs rained down overhead, pulverizing their homes. In 2024, Israeli forces targeting Hamas terrorists obliterated much of neighboring Gaza, displacing millions of people. News reports showed charred apartment buildings, crippled hospitals, and people desperate for food, clean water, and medical care. These scenes can help us imagine just how horrible the destruction of Jerusalem must have been.

The prophet Jeremiah, who lived in Judah and prophesied to God's people, looked out over the city and cried,

> What can I say for you, to what compare you,
>   O daughter of Jerusalem?
> What can I liken to you, that I may comfort you,
>   O virgin daughter of Zion?

> For your ruin is vast as the sea;
> who can heal you? (Lamentations 2:13 ESV)

Your ruin is vast as the sea. What once was radiant is now ruin. What once shone like the sun smolders. A city, God's Holy City, the City of David, once filled with God's people, had been cast down and trampled under the feet of the nations.

God had warned his people through the words of his prophets. "Return to me," he told them time and again. "I see you attempting to look religious while your heart is far from me. I am God and there is no other. I am the God of your fathers—of Abraham, Isaac, and Jacob. I am the one who delivered you from Egypt and established you in this land. I am the one who chose you to be my treasured possession, my light to the nations. But you refuse to worship me" (see Deuteronomy 8; Jeremiah 16–17; 25; and Ezekiel 4; 7–11).

And so ruin came. Her name was Babylon. Nebuchadnezzar, king of Babylon, laid siege to Jerusalem. His army surrounded the city—creating fear and famine within her. Eventually, the wall was breached. Judah's fighting men fled, and Zedekiah the king was captured. But the worst was still to come. Babylon had taken Judah's king, but now they would seek to take her very heart and soul. The commander of Nebuchadnezzar's imperial guard, Nebuzaradan, came to Jerusalem to take up the task of utter destruction. Jeremiah described it this way: "He set fire to the temple of the LORD, the royal palace and all the houses of Jerusalem. Every important building he burned down. The whole Babylonian army, under the commander of the imperial guard, broke down all the walls around Jerusalem" (Jeremiah 52:13-14). Many of the remaining people were carried off into exile in Babylon.

EXAMINING THE BROKEN PIECES

Jeremiah had the opportunity to go to Babylon with the exiles, but he chose to stay behind in Jerusalem and survey the damage. He looked carefully at all of the broken pieces. And this is how he responded: "How lonely sits the city" once so "full of people" (see Lamentations 1:1 ESV). Many of us have seen lonely cities in recent memory. We remember the quiet streets and empty buildings during the first months of the Covid-19 pandemic. But Jeremiah's city wasn't only lonely; it had been utterly destroyed. Imagine every brick toppled and charred, every stone cast down like a scene in an apocalyptic thriller. "All the splendor has departed from Daughter Zion," Jeremiah wrote (Lamentations 1:6).

We know what he saw, but how did Jeremiah feel when he looked out at all of the damage? He wrote in Lamentations,

> This is why I weep
>   and my eyes overflow with tears.
> No one is near to comfort me,
>   no one to restore my spirit. (Lamentations 1:16)

> My eyes fail from weeping,
>   I am in torment within;
> My heart is poured out on the ground
>   because my people are destroyed,
> because children and infants faint
>   in the streets of the city. (Lamentations 2:11)

What could Jeremiah do but cry?

EXAMINING OUR BROKEN PIECES

You might be wondering what the destruction of Jerusalem has to do with the disappointment, disillusionment, and devastation we experience in our work. The two scenarios seem worlds apart. Jerusalem's destruction came because of the people's sin and refusal to turn back to God. Some issues we experience at work may be our fault, but much of the hurt we experience in the workplace happens because of broken people operating in broken systems. But the two scenarios have something significant in common: immense pain that can wreak havoc on our lives. The destruction of Jerusalem and the hurt we experience at work cut to the core of our beings.

Work hurt can cause both acute and chronic pain. The acute pain is the type that comes out of nowhere. It levels you because it seems sudden and severe. In an essay for *Harvard Business Review* on managing emotions at work, Vasundhara Sawhney recalled a time when she received an unexpected blow from her boss:

> Ten years ago, on what could've been a perfect Friday evening, my boss shamed me in front of my entire team. "Isn't this something we discussed a few months ago? Why wasn't the protocol followed?" he screamed. . . . Angry and humiliated, I excused myself from the meeting and charged toward the elevator. I made the trip five floors down to the parking lot. Then I sat in my car and cried.[11]

Clearly this interaction with her boss in front of her team was distressful. Her boss's words emotionally wrecked her. The meeting had become unsafe because her boss had inflicted pain, and she needed to get out of there. Her flight response kicked in and got her from that meeting all the way down to her car, where it felt safe to cry.

Work hurt can also cause chronic pain—the pain that lingers. It's dull and persistent. It's the shame that lasts long after being belittled by your supervisor, the unemployment that persists after you've been laid off, and the disrespect that your organization continually communicates through low pay.

One way that chronic pain manifests is burnout. Burnout has been recognized by the World Health Organization as an occupational health issue. Let's take a look at their definition:

> Burn-out is a syndrome conceptualized as resulting from chronic workplace stress that has not been successfully managed. It is characterized by three dimensions:

1. feelings of energy depletion or exhaustion;
2. increased mental distance from one's job, or feelings of negativism or cynicism related to one's job; and
3. reduced professional efficacy.[12]

Sisters Emily and Amelia Nagoski, in their book *Burnout: The Secret to Unlocking the Stress Cycle*, focus on the emotional exhaustion component of burnout, citing its drastic impact on our health. They connect the emotional exhaustion to not being able to move through some of the negative emotions we experience in the midst of our work: "Sometimes we get stuck because we can't find our way through," they write. "The most difficult feelings—rage, grief, despair, helplessness—may be too treacherous to move through alone."[13] It's that stuck-ness that makes the work hurt chronic.

Unfortunately, I know a few people who have experienced burnout as a result of chronic pain, stress, and frustration at work. Just as chronic back pain can make everyday activities feel unthinkable, chronic work pain can be absolutely debilitating. Those working in helping professions are particularly prone to burnout and its kin, compassion fatigue. I've already mentioned that K-12 teachers top the list in terms of most burned-out professionals. But let's talk about nurses. The National Council of State Boards of Nursing found that, in the United States, about one hundred thousand nurses left the workforce during the pandemic because of stress, burnout, retirement, or some combination of these.[14] If that's not grim, check out these numbers: "A quarter to half of nurses reported feeling emotionally drained (50.8%), used up (56.4%), fatigued (49.7%), burned out (45.1%), or at the end of the rope (29.4%) 'a few times a week' or 'every day.'"[15]

> *Just as chronic back pain can make everyday activities feel unthinkable, chronic work pain can be absolutely debilitating.*

My guess is that most folks who train to be teachers and nurses do so because they want to help people. That's why I wanted to become a teacher. Teachers want to make a difference in the lives of their students. Nurses want to provide care and ease suffering. Many nurses and teachers feel a sense of calling to their work and derive profound personal meaning from it. Brian, an elementary school teacher, told me that quitting his job felt so painful because his identity was tied up in his work. He was a teacher. He had trained to be a teacher. And if he was no longer a teacher, what was he? That's why it can hurt so badly when the work we love has knocked us down—and even knocked some of us completely out of the profession.

IT'S OKAY TO CRY

When work causes pain—whether acute or chronic—perhaps the first thing we need to know is that it's okay to cry. That's what we can learn from Jeremiah. When the walls fall down, it's okay to take some time to survey the damage—the damage done to our hearts, our careers, our livelihood—and feel absolutely broken. It's okay to grieve. It's okay to say to the Lord,

"It hurt when my teammates spread that rumor about me."

"It hurt when I lost my job."

"I feel ashamed when I look at my résumé."

"I'm worried that I won't be able to get another job."

"I'm sick and tired of employers not seeing the value I bring to the table."

"My boss's lack of empathy toward me made me feel alone."

"I didn't know people could be so hateful."

Jeremiah's sad words, his lamentations, remind us that it's okay to bring our heartbreak to God. It's okay to bring every disappointment, every instance that disillusions us, every moment that devastates us to him. In fact, God welcomes our pain.[16] The psalmist reminds us, "The LORD is close to the brokenhearted" (Psalm 34:18). God doesn't need for us to resolve our pain, to be all whole and healed in order to faithfully follow him. God comes near to us in our pain.

And God comforts us. The how and the when are somewhat of a mystery. But in his mercy, God can transform our pain. The apostle Paul calls God "the Father of compassion and the God of all comfort" (2 Corinthians 1:3). Paul goes on to tell us why God comforts us: "so that we can comfort those in any trouble with the comfort we ourselves receive from God" (2 Corinthians 1:4). God comforts us because he loves us *and* so that we can extend compassion to others who are hurting.

When we tell God about our pain through our groans and our cries, we're asking him to do something about it because we believe he cares for us. We believe that God is the author of a story of redemption in which the ending involves no more tears and no more pain (Revelation 21:4). And we want—we *need*—to experience a taste of that redemption when work hurts.

A LAMENT FOR WHEN WORK KNOCKS US DOWN

When work knocks us down, the temptation can be to quickly begin to pick up the pieces. But the invitation here is for us to survey the damage first and bring our pain to God, to tell God how many ways work has beaten us up, burned us out, and broken our hearts, and to tell God that the walls have fallen down and that we're sitting in a pile of ruin and rubble. I encourage you to make a list of the ways work has disappointed, disillusioned, and even devastated you. Be gentle and patient with yourself while making this list. The work of remembering could resurface the pain.

Remember what Richard Rohr said, "If we do not transform our pain, we will most assuredly transmit it." Here's the first step in the transformation: Bring your pain to God. Acknowledge your pain knowing that God sees it too. You can write in your journal about all of the damage work has caused. Or you can head out to the tennis court and send every ball over the net with the intensity of the

> *Bring your pain to God. Acknowledge your pain knowing that God sees it too.*

emotional pain, social pain, and financial pain you've endured, each hit with the racket, a prayer. Talk with a friend about the shame and humiliation you've experienced. Paint a picture that captures the loneliness and estrangement that come from being unemployed. Punch your pillow when you feel overwhelmed by the loss of income and your fears about being able to pay your rent.

As you do, cry. Groan. Shake your fist in the air. Because this is not the way work is supposed to be. Then ask God to bring you comfort. Ask God to extend his compassion to you. As you bring your pain to God, know that he loves you. God delights in you, and he wants you to flourish. It may still take some time to pick up the pieces—but this is where we start.

WORK HURT CLINIC

Symptoms: Which of the following have you experienced in your work? List specific examples, if possible.
- Disappointment
- Disillusionment
- Devastation

Causes: As you reflect on the disappointment, disillusionment, and devastation in your work, reflect on . . .
- expectations that weren't met;
- assumptions that were challenged; and
- times you felt helpless, overwhelmed, or completely destroyed.

Care:
- Bring your pain to God in a way that makes sense for you.
- Ask God to be compassionate toward you.
- Remember that God loves you.

2

Feeling like an Exile

"WORK WAS LITERALLY KILLING ME," Mina remarked. Just a few months before, she had been in the hospital under stroke watch following a series of severe and sudden headaches. Doctors hospitalized her for brain inflammation and observed her closely for days. While she was lying in her hospital bed, even the slightest thought of what she had been experiencing at work made her blood pressure skyrocket and her head hurt. She reflected, "My body was telling me, 'Get the hell out of here.'"

Mina needed to leave the company she cofounded with Angela in 2017. At first, they worked well together, close friends bonded by a shared vision. Angela oversaw the company's vision and strategy while Mina took responsibility for the operations and staff. In 2023, their relationship began to erode. Mina likened it to a joint in which the cartilage had worn away.

Mina suspected that Angela wasn't operating in good faith. She felt that some of the speaking and consulting gigs Angela had been accepting were taking potential clients and profits from their company. How could they expect to close deals with these clients after Angela did business with them on her own? Just thinking about the conflict brewing between them overwhelmed Mina. In a board meeting Mina lost it. Enough was enough. She needed the board to create some clarity around Angela's activities, but she sensed they were unwilling to intervene.

A few weeks after the board meeting, Mina and Angela agreed to take their issues to an organizational coach they had been working with so that he could help them engage in constructive dialogue and problem-solving. Much to Mina's surprise, on the day of the meeting, Angela began the meeting by telling the consultant that Mina had acted inappropriately in the board meeting and that her behaviors constituted a fireable offense. Mina couldn't believe her ears. She was humiliated. *Why hadn't Angela brought this up with her before in a one-on-one?* she wondered. Mina said she felt like she was being punished, as if Angela were retaliating against her for raising questions about the speaking and consulting engagements. Mina explained, "It felt mean."

From that point, Mina and Angela's relationship continued to deteriorate. Even though they had been business partners for years, Angela began harshly criticizing Mina's work: "You're terrible at finances. You shouldn't be in operations." Mina had trouble reconciling that feedback with what she had heard from some of their clients and external vendors, some who affirmed her by saying she should work in a Fortune 500 company. Angela also started questioning Mina's ability to fulfill her responsibilities given Mina's season of life as a young mom. Mina was dumbfounded. Then Angela suggested that Mina quit.

A week later, the headaches started. Mina had been burnt out before, and she had been diligent about practicing self-care and maintaining her boundaries. But this was more than burnout. Mina knew she needed to quit her job. But every time she thought about how to leave well, she would get another headache. A friend helped her see that she had three options: she could stay and be a team player, use her voice, or exit.[1] Mina had been a team player. She had used her voice to advocate for change. It was time to leave, and she

Feeling like an Exile

didn't need one last hurrah before she went. She couldn't. Work was killing her.

Mina left the company, and while the company gave her a very generous severance package, her losses were overwhelming. In addition to losing her income, she lost her sense of ambition, the dreams she had for the company, and her status in the business community. She lost her relationships with her colleagues and with the staff she had hired and cared for. She lost the rhythm and organization of her days. She was out of work, removed from previously life-giving relationships, and excused from a leadership development cohort she and Angela had joined together. She found herself at home, alone, exiled from a work life she had once loved.

Work hurt can cause us to feel like an exile. The good news is that we can turn to the story of the Israelites, who were exiled from their homeland, to learn how to cope when we find ourselves displaced, feeling separated from all we once held dear.

> *We can turn to the story of the Israelites, who were exiled from their homeland, to learn how to cope when we find ourselves displaced.*

After the walls fell down in Jerusalem, the people of Judah didn't have time to change into their sweats and start eating their feelings, because the Babylonians took many of them into exile. This was forced captivity. But it was also God's punishment. God had warned his people that exile would be the consequence of their continued sin. God used Jeremiah to speak this warning to Judah:

> Therefore the LORD Almighty says this: "Because you have not listened to my words, I will summon all the peoples of the north and my servant Nebuchadnezzar king of Babylon," declares the LORD, "and I will bring them against this land and

its inhabitants and against all the surrounding nations. I will completely destroy them and make them an object of horror and scorn, and an everlasting ruin. I will banish from them the sounds of joy and gladness, the voices of bride and bridegroom, the sound of millstones and the light of the lamp. This whole country will become a desolate wasteland, and these nations will serve the king of Babylon seventy years." (Jeremiah 25:8-11)

What could they take with them besides what little they had left and their grief?

More grief, as it turns out. For many of the Israelites who went into exile, their pain didn't stop when the Babylonians destroyed Jerusalem. In some ways, it had only just begun. They experienced pain in Babylon and still had challenges when they returned home to Jerusalem. The same can be true for us when work breaks our hearts. The knocks just keep coming, often in the form of the displacements we experience as a result.

DISPLACEMENTS

In *Compassion: A Reflection on the Christian Life,* Henri Nouwen and his coauthors Donald McNeill and Douglas Morrison use the word *displacement* to describe a situation in which we find ourselves dislocated. Displacement can be involuntary, such as the case of being exiled from or forced out of one's country, or voluntary, such as choosing to move to a new city. And displacement isn't just physical, or geographical. Nouwen, McNeill, and Morrison write about the inner displacements we experience—those situations that make us feel mentally or emotionally distanced from what we previously knew or what felt comfortable and at home. "We do not have to look very long or far to find displacements in our lives," they write.[2]

If we pause for a moment, perhaps we can think of a few displacements we've experienced. One of my biggest displacements resulted from a voluntary move to Chicago for grad school. I grew up in Alabama and went to college in Tennessee. Apart from a few summer jobs, I had never really lived anywhere but the southeastern United States. Culturally, the Southeast and the North Shore of Chicago are more than seven hundred miles apart. When I arrived in Illinois in 2003, I had a cute southern accent, but I dialed it back so people wouldn't think I was dumb. And, bless my heart, I asked a lady at a department store if a wool pea coat would keep me warm in winters. She laughed and told me it would be a good fall jacket. Yikes!

Moving to Chicago, I felt like I was following in the footsteps of one of my favorite authors, Rick Bragg. We had studied his memoir *All Over but the Shoutin'* in my Southern Literature class in college, and the theme of "exiled to the north" was one idea from my professor's lectures that stuck with me. Bragg grew up in Alabama and decided to go into journalism. His career eventually landed him at the *New York Times*. New York felt so foreign to him. But what's worse, his Alabama home started to feel a bit foreign as well. That's what happened to me. Along with the physical displacement came some emotional displacement as well. I was the only member of my extended family who moved up north. Because I lived so far away, I missed family gatherings like birthday parties and baby showers. And then I went and married a Yankee, as my grandmother liked to describe him. Home started to feel both physically and emotionally distant.

Displacement—no matter the cause or the form—can be extremely painful. Walter Wangerin Jr. describes the relational displacement that can result from moving to a new place: "We are woven into communities, though we may be unconscious of the webbing that supports us—the shopkeepers, neighbors, church families—until we move to another town. And then we become terribly conscious, because of the breaking. A thousand tiny *snaps!*"[3] Wangerin likens this sort of displacement to a death: "Someone did die. You, at displacement. And the period of distress, the overwhelming sense of vulnerability and loneliness and even the heavy lethargy that follows, are natural after all."[4] When work hurt causes our displacement, we can feel the same level of grief and loss.

In Venezuela, Jorge was a successful executive with degrees in business and marketing. One of his passions was seeing and developing the potential in others. He had a knack for understanding people. He absolutely loved hiring good people and then seeing them do well in their roles.

> *Someone did die. You, at displacement.*
> **WALTER WANGERIN JR.**

When Jorge immigrated to the United States to be with his wife, he could not read, write, or understand English. Yet he needed a job. So he worked in a warehouse and drove for Uber. All of his adult life he had been an independent businessman; he worked because he loved it. In his new country, he worked because he had to. He told his wife he was miserable. He never expected to be a laborer, and he didn't want to be stuck in these stopgap jobs for years. Jorge longed to be in a job where he could put his gifts and skills to work. He couldn't use them in the warehouse or in the car. He felt like he was wasting his time. He wanted to return to his home country.

We can experience both voluntary and involuntary displacements in our work. Walking away from a job is one form of voluntary displacement. But many of the displacements we encounter are involuntary. We don't ask to be disappointed, disillusioned, or devastated in our work. We don't seek out the toxic boss, the sexual harassment, the racial discrimination, or the layoff.

Those involuntary displacements can also cause physical displacements. When we lose our job, we may no longer have a commute or go into an office every day. We may even be forced to leave the neighborhood or city we were in, to find a new job or a more affordable rent. But most of the displacements we experience, in our work, are of the inner variety. There are three main types of inner displacement we can experience when work breaks our hearts—vocational, relational, and spiritual.

VOCATIONAL DISPLACEMENT

First, certain forms of work-related heartbreak can leave us feeling vocationally displaced. In modern English, the word *vocation* has become synonymous with "profession" or "occupation." But historically the word meant a call or summons from God to a particular type of work. Here I'm going to use it both ways. To be vocationally displaced is to have lost sight of our career trajectory or our sense of calling. Some of us feel displaced when we're knocked off our career path.

After she closed Joy Village School, Lora needed to find a new job. She had debts to pay and a family to help support. She found a new role fairly quickly, but every day she wrestled with questions of identity and purpose: *Who am I? Why am I getting up in the morning? What am I here for? Why am I here in this office doing things that don't feel significant?* She questioned her calling to start the school: *Did I hear that right?* Her child even asked her, "Why did God ask you to do that if it was only going to be for a year?" Lora told me, "I felt embarrassed because I had been putting this narrative out into the community that God was doing this. When it ended, I felt like an impostor. Maybe I was wrong." She wondered what else she could be good at.

Vocational displacement also occurs when the heartbreaks we experience in our work make us feel like we've lost our sense of calling. Let's think of calling as an invitation from God to use the gifts and resources he's given us to partner in his redemptive work in the world. When work disappoints us, it can make us wonder if we missed our calling in the first place. Were we wrong? Or did we just discern really poorly?

I think this doubt creeps up because, somehow, we've come to believe that working in line with our sense of calling should exempt us from experiencing hardship or suffering. But if the stories of

God's people tell us anything, it's that we should expect struggles (John 16:33). The goal is not to let the struggles overcome us. Our calling is bigger than any job. Difficult circumstances don't necessarily negate a calling. But they may propel us into a season of discernment in which we have to locate our calling, our sense of purpose, buried in all the rubble.

RELATIONAL DISPLACEMENT

The second kind of internal displacement work hurt can cause is relational displacement, which manifests in a variety of ways. Sometimes the grief we experience at work results in relational separation. When we quit or lose a job, we may automatically lose the connections we had with our coworkers. Proximity is a powerful component of relationships. When you no longer go into the office or log on to the weekly Zoom meeting, it can be challenging to maintain the friendships you had at work. Almost immediately, you become an outsider.

Toxic work situations can also cause relational strife. My husband worked for a narcissistic pastor who had a group of "yes men" elders around him who affirmed the pastor's every word and deed. When my husband shared some of his concerns about the pastor with these elders, the elders sided with the pastor and left my husband feeling alone—like he was the only one seeing the red flags. Both relational strife and separation can leave us feeling isolated.

Our inability to talk about our work hurt and the ensuing grief can also make us feel displaced. Brené Brown notes that both our inability to communicate well about our grief and our culture's tendency to move on quickly from difficult circumstances can create feelings of isolation. She writes, "The more difficult it is for us to articulate our experiences of loss, longing, and feeling lost to the people around us, the more disconnected and alone we feel. Talking about grief is difficult in a world that wants us to 'get over it' or a community that is quick to pathologize grief."[5]

Feeling like an Exile

In her book *This Too Shall Last: Finding Grace When Suffering Lingers*, K.J. Ramsey looks through the lens of the Christian faith at our culture's tendency to avoid grief and wisely asserts:

> We've so fused our American Dream with the risen Christ that when suffering enters our lives and does not leave quickly, all we know how to do is hide, judge, or despair. We've reduced the gospel to rescue, power to privilege, and hope to swift healing, reducing ourselves in the process. Western Christianity has long treated suffering like a problem to fix and a blight to hide.... When our storylines do not match the arc of triumph we've come to expect and revere, we can feel stuck on the outside of both our communities and God's grace.[6]

For the longest time, I had trouble talking about some of my work heartbreak, especially with friends who seemed to have wonderful jobs and appeared to have effortlessly climbed the career ladder. I was ashamed. I didn't think they would understand. My inability to communicate what I had experienced and how terrible it made me feel cut me off from the love and support I so desperately needed. Rachel felt similarly when she was laid off from her job. Two weeks later, she had told very few people. "I felt so embarrassed," she said. Our pain can leave us feeling utterly alone in the times we most need compassion and grace.

SPIRITUAL DISPLACEMENT

Feeling lost can accompany grief, but it's also a consequence, a ripple effect, something that happens one click past simultaneously. Unmet hopes, imploded assumptions, and unexpected jilts can affect our inner compass. For those of us whose faith provides our orienting framework and for whom Jesus is our North Star, work hurt can raise some serious questions about God and our walk with him. This is what I call *spiritual displacement*.

> For those of us whose faith provides our orienting framework and for whom Jesus is our North Star, work hurt can raise some serious questions about God and our walk with him.

K.J. Ramsey wrote of grief, "We can feel stuck on the outside of both our communities and God's grace." On the outside of God's grace? When work breaks our hearts, we can experience a sense of separation from God. Could we be angry at him for allowing it to happen? Could we be questioning his goodness because we're in pain? When suffering from work-related hurt, it's not uncommon to enter a time of wrestling with God. We have to work out once again what it means to follow God even when we might experience pain.

DISPLACEMENT AND EXILE

All of these displacements are their own mini exiles. To be sure, it's unlikely that devastation at work will result in someone removing us from our homes, from everything we've ever known, but nevertheless we do experience an exile of sorts. According to Nouwen and friends, even these types of displacements have the potential to turn us toward despair and spite: "In our modern society with its increasing mobility and pluriformity, we have become the subjects and often the victims of so many displacements that it is very hard to keep a sense of rootedness, and we are constantly tempted to become bitter and resentful."[7]

Once again, we can turn to the experiences of God's people to learn how to keep going after work causes painful displacements. After the walls fell down in Jerusalem, many of the Israelites were carried off into Babylon. Perhaps we can find a little solidarity with those who watched Jerusalem's destruction and then, while their grief was still fresh, got jilted straight out of Judah.

JILTED OUT OF JUDAH

Abruptly losing your job is bad. I can't imagine losing my home, my place of worship, the halls of government, as well as family and friends. War with Babylon left the people of Jerusalem starving, defeated, and sorting through piles of stone and ash. But they couldn't sit in the rubble forever. Many of them had to get up and get moving . . . to Babylon. God had warned his people that their disobedience and failure to return to him would result in their ruin.[8] And God kept that promise.

Babylon carried the people of Judah into exile. Both 2 Kings and Jeremiah record, "So Judah went into captivity, away from her land" (2 Kings 25:21; Jeremiah 52:27). The Babylonians took the royal family, their advisers, craftsmen, and artisans (Jeremiah 29:2). They left some of the poorest and weakest behind in Jerusalem because they wouldn't pose any real threat to the new ruling nation. Over the course of sixteen years, Nebuchadnezzar carried thousands of Israelites into exile.

The Israelites living in Judah lost practically everything, and then the Babylonians carried them off into a foreign land. God physically removed them from their city. He relocated them in a polytheistic culture while they still were riddled with grief. And yet they clung to God and to each other to make sense of it all, to feel anchored amid the chaos, to feel held even in times when they felt very, very alone.

No one book of the Bible gives us a detailed account of the Babylonian captivity. Instead, we get a few glimpses of what it was like from Psalms and the Prophets. We know that not everyone experienced the exile the same way. Some carried profound grief and anger with them into captivity. Some faced enormous challenges that tested their faith. Others experienced distress in the midst of exile and needed the comfort of God. Regardless of their different experiences, these people shared something—their desire for community, their need for the nearness of God, and their belief in the sovereignty of God. We see all of this in their prayers.

PRAYERS OF THE PEOPLE

Let's start with the book of Daniel. The events recorded in this book took place during the time of the Babylonian exile, and some of its most familiar stories have wisdom for us for when we're feeling displaced. These stories remind us that when we experience work hurt, we can turn to God in prayer and be reminded of both God's sovereignty and God's nearness.

Daniel, Hananiah, Mishael, and Azariah were the cream of the crop among the young men of Judah. Nebuchadnezzar appointed them to service in his palace, which required them to learn the Babylonian culture and language (Daniel 1:3-6). These four young men were taken captive in Judah, brought to Babylon, and then enrolled in the training program for those destined to join the king's service. The Bible doesn't tell us if these young men felt profound grief in the wake of the exile or when they found themselves in their new roles. But we know that living in Babylon tested their faith.

> *The stories of the Babylonian exiles remind us that when we experience work hurt, we can turn to God in prayer and be reminded of both God's sovereignty and God's nearness.*

Mighty conquering king Nebuchadnezzar had troubling dreams. He wanted his astrologers to interpret them, but they couldn't. That made Nebuchadnezzar so raging mad that he wanted to execute all the wise men of Babylon, including Daniel and his three friends (Daniel 2:12-13). But Daniel and his friends didn't want to be executed, so Daniel asked for the opportunity to interpret Nebuchadnezzar's dream. The Bible tells us that God "gave knowledge and understanding of all kinds of literature and learning" to Daniel and his friends (Daniel 1:17). God also gave Daniel the gift of being able to understand visions and dreams (Daniel 1:17).

Nebuchadnezzar agreed to let Daniel try his dream-interpretation skills, and that's when Daniel and his friends started praying. "[Daniel] urged them to plead for mercy from the God of heaven concerning this mystery, so that he and his friends might not be executed with the rest of the wise men of Babylon" (Daniel 2:18). Daniel didn't pray alone. He turned to other God-followers and they prayed together. We don't know exactly what Daniel and his friends prayed, but we have a sense of the content of their prayer. They needed God's mercy and help with a particular problem— understanding the king's dream. They wanted God to intervene in their immediate circumstances. They desperately needed God's nearness.

But they also kept God's sovereignty in view. God was merciful and answered their prayer. He gave Daniel the key to the dream, and Daniel erupted in a prayer of praise.

> Praise be to the name of God for ever and ever;
>   wisdom and power are his.
> He changes times and seasons;
>   he deposes kings and raises up others.
> He gives wisdom to the wise
>   and knowledge to the discerning.
> He reveals deep and hidden things;
>   he knows what lies in darkness,
>   and light dwells with him.
> I thank and praise you, God of my ancestors:
>   You have given me wisdom and power,
> you have made known to me what we asked of you,

you have made known to us the dream of the king.
(Daniel 2:20-23)

Daniel's prayer celebrated God's power and rule.

Let's look at another prayer—this one is recorded in Psalms. The *Africa Bible Commentary* introduction to this psalm notes, "The exile was a time of grief and distress, when the people were moved to pray earnestly for God's judgment on their enemies."[9] The psalm begins by giving us a picture of a group of exiles grieving together.

> By the rivers of Babylon we sat and wept
> when we remembered Zion. (Psalm 137:1)

The psalm continues,

> There on the poplars
> we hung our harps,
> for there our captors asked us for songs,
> our tormentors demanded songs of joy;
> they said, "Sing us one of the songs of Zion!" (Psalm 137:1-3)

The Israelites carried their grief with them into exile. The Babylonians' jeers compounded their heartache. It was hard enough to sing their songs of praise "while in a foreign land" (Psalm 137:4). These exiles longed for their beloved Jerusalem, and the taunting of the Babylonians only made it worse. That triggered what the *Africa Bible Commentary* describes as "a terrible prayer."[10]

These were the people who prayed,

> Daughter Babylon, doomed to destruction,
> happy is the one who repays you
> according to what you have done to us.
> Happy is the one who seizes your infants
> and dashes them against the rocks. (Psalm 137:8-9)

We may see the words, "Happy is the one" and think that this psalm is telling us about the blessed life—like an ancient Beatitude. Nope.

This is actually a prayer for God's judgment on his enemies. In that "happy is the one" line, God's people were talking about how good it would make them feel to see Babylonian babies dying. Pretty raw in terms of grief and emotion.

But still, we can see in this prayer that the exiles found comfort in their memory of being together in Jerusalem. They prayed for God's nearness—"Remember, Lord," they prayed (Psalm 137:7). They also trusted in God's sovereignty. Only in sticking together, in believing in God's nearness and trusting in his supreme rule over the heavens and the earth, could the Israelites endure the exile.

Let's look at one final prayer, a prayer of lament: Psalm 102. We don't know many details about this one, but we can discern that it was written during the Babylonian exile based on the psalmist's reference to the destruction of Jerusalem. The psalmist begins by petitioning the Lord in Psalm 102:1-2, wanting God to be attentive to his affliction and his distress. He needs God's nearness *now*. Next, the psalmist offers a vivid description of the emotional, physical, and social toll the distress has taken on him.

> For my days vanish like smoke;
>   my bones burn like glowing embers.
> My heart is blighted and withered like grass;
>   I forget to eat my food.
> In my distress I groan aloud
>   and am reduced to skin and bones.
> I am like a desert owl,
>   like an owl among the ruins.
> I lie awake; I have become
>   like a bird alone on a roof.
> All day long my enemies taunt me;
>   those who rail against me use my name as a curse.
> (Psalm 102:3-8)

The psalmist knew that the Lord had a hand in his distress. "For I eat ashes as my food and mingle my drink with tears because of your great wrath" (Psalm 102:9-10). But he also believed that the Lord was sovereign and compassionate (Psalm 102:12-17). The Lord was near to people, like him, who are brokenhearted (cf. Psalm 34:18).

Even in the midst of his sadness, his affliction, his grief, his distress, the psalmist could proclaim to the Lord,

> In the beginning you laid the foundations of the earth,
>   and the heavens are the work of your hands.
> They will perish, but you remain;
>   they will all wear out like a garment.
> Like clothing you will change them
>   and they will be discarded.
> But you remain the same,
>   and your years will never end.
> The children of your servants will live in your presence;
>   their descendants will be established before you.
>   (Psalm 102:25-28)

The Lord remains. He is faithful. He is steadfast. He is our fortress and our refuge, our ever-present help in time of need (Psalm 46:1) even when we have seen our physical fortress—the city of Jerusalem—reduced to dust.

The community piece is less apparent in this prayer. We don't see much evidence of the psalmist turning to his fellow exiles in his distress. Instead, the psalmist has a longer view of the role of community in navigating hard times. He wants future generations of God's people to find strength from his experience and his words. He prays, "Let this be written for a future generation, that a people not yet created may praise the LORD" (Psalm 102:18). God allowed the Babylonians to crush the walls of Jerusalem. The psalmist's heart, his very bones felt crushed under the weight of his grief and distress. He carried with him the memories of his beloved city, now reduced to rubble. And yet he focused on the future generations. He wanted them to know the faithfulness of the Lord. He wanted to be part of their "great cloud of witnesses," encouraging them to persevere in the midst of hardship (Hebrews 12:1).

WHEN WE FEEL LIKE AN EXILE

When work beats us up, it's easy to feel like an exile. We carry our pain, shame, and anger with us, along with our vocational, relational, or spiritual displacement. The story of the exiles tells us that the keys to survival are community and belonging, God's nearness and comfort, and a radical reorientation to God's sovereign care.

Leaning into community and belonging, waiting for God's nearness and comfort, and seeing ourselves under God's sovereign care takes effort and intentionality. It requires some initiative on our part when all we really want to do is sit in the rubble and lick our wounds. So what do we do? How do we find community and belonging when grief isolates and alienates us? How can we feel God's nearness and comfort when we feel far from him? And how can we fix our eyes on Jesus, the author and perfector of our faith, when the world feels like it's spinning out of control?

Tell somebody. First, if we're going to eat our feelings, we might as well do it with a friend. We need to talk about our pain and frustration even though it feels risky. We may have to overcome some shame and our pride to tell someone how work broke our hearts. The people we share with might not understand our situation, and they might not respond with the compassion we need and desire. But we can't go it alone. The story of the exiles reminds us that we need others to help us make it through. We need them to sing songs of God's faithfulness when the words fail us. We need them to hold us up when all we want to do is sit down on the ground and cry. Community can begin to counteract the relational displacement we feel when work hurts us.

Keeping our hurt to ourselves is not an option. We need compassion from another human being we can see and hear and touch. We need eyes that see, ears that listen, and arms that embrace. And it may take us a few difficult conversations to find empathy. But that shared understanding grounds us and reminds us that, even though we're feeling displaced, we are not alone.

So maybe it starts with a short text or phone call—saying the words before they've fully registered. *I lost my job. I think I was just sexually harassed by my boss. I didn't realize people could be so mean.* That movement toward someone, however small, is a step toward community. It's a plea for love. It's a cry for solidarity and belonging. It's the hope for compassion.

Tell God. We also need to turn toward God. We need to talk to him about our situation. We need to be real with God about our pain. Did you see how honest the author of Psalm 102 was about his pain—about the physical, emotional, and social toll it had taken? We need to tell God about all of it. But we also need to tell God about the fallout. The grief has not gone away. It has only grown. So too should our prayers multiply.

While we're being real with God about our heartache, we also need to ask for his help. As I've looked at other prayers of lament, I've noticed how often the writers ask God to look, see, hear, and remember. They, like Daniel and his friends, believed that God cares about our circumstances and can intervene in them. We need to pray boldly, petitioning God to come near. Reaching out to God can shrink the chasm of spiritual displacement.

Remember that God is sovereign. Finally, we need to keep God's sovereignty in mind. We have to remember that he has the whole world in his hands. Not even a sparrow can fall to the ground without his knowledge (Matthew 10:29). So you better believe that when work has broken your heart, that God sees you and cares for you even as he's orchestrating the affairs of the universe. Remembering who God is and that we are his handiwork created in Christ

Jesus to do good works (see Ephesians 2:10) calls us out of vocational displacement. It gives us hope that God will bring beauty out of the ashes in his time.

ON THE OTHER SIDE OF DISPLACEMENT

Displacement didn't derail Jorge. Even though he hated his jobs in the warehouse and driving for Uber, he worked hard. His abuela instilled that value in him. Jorge drew on his entrepreneurial skills to overcome the frustration he felt in his jobs. With the support of his wife and other family members, he committed himself to learning the language and the culture of his new home. He also began to help his in-laws' businesses. Now he's seeing the fruits of his efforts: he is adapting to life in the United States and reengaging in work he loves. And he doesn't miss Venezuela anymore.

Laney is also learning to live on the other side of displacement caused by work hurt.

When work hurt happens in a church, the vocational, relational, and spiritual displacement that result can be pronounced because, for many church workers, their workplace is also their community. Laney had attended her church for eight years and had been on staff for five overseeing the small groups ministry. As a single woman, she found a sense of home with several of the families in the church who loved her, and she loved her job.

After she had been on staff for three years, the church got a new senior pastor. Without seeking Laney's input, this pastor changed the format of the weekly small groups. Then he moved Laney out of her position and into a new role that she didn't enjoy. Disapproving of many of the changes the new pastor instituted, families Laney loved began leaving. Sunday mornings became days filled with loss and sadness as the people she loved no longer walked through the church doors. Eventually, the church closed. During the final worship service, Laney wept, unable to contain her heartbreak. She was losing her job and community, and she had to face difficult questions about her future.

In the months that followed, Laney relied on severance to cover her bills while she sought healing and a new job. She went to therapy. She went to job interviews. And when she had the courage, she went to church. Her friends had scattered to several churches in the area, but she would join them in worship. They would embrace, encourage one another, and together sing their praise as if strangers in a foreign land, all the while remembering the goodness of God.

WORK HURT CLINIC

Symptoms: Which of the following have you experienced as the result of work hurt?
- Vocational displacement
- Relational displacement
- Spiritual displacement

Causes: What do you think contributed to the displacement you felt?
- Losing your sense of calling
- Being knocked off your career trajectory
- Losing contact with colleagues
- Moving to a new place
- Not sharing your grief with others
- Working in a new environment
- Doubting God's goodness
- Questioning God's love for you

Care:
- Tell someone about your work hurt.
- Tell God about your work hurt.
- Remember that God is sovereign.

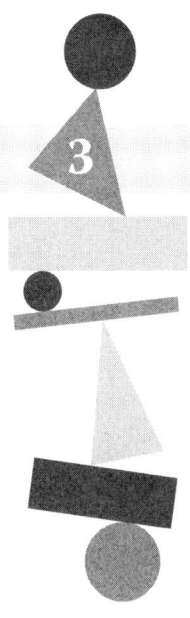

3

Learning to See in the Dark

WHEN IT COMES TO DISAPPOINTMENT, disillusionment, and devastation, Jason hit the trifecta. His story could be inspiration for the next TV law office drama, and it's a story that's still going. He's still taking the blows, but he's still standing. Jason is a creative who designs and develops virtual worlds for video games. He founded his company with the hope of doing good work and treating his employees well.

After running his business by himself for a few years, Jason invited two friends to become his business partners. Initially they worked well together. But over time, these business partners began to devalue Jason's creative contributions, business insight, and vision for company values. Staging a takeover, Jason's partners started receiving coaching from external consultants and began to use some questionable business practices. In 2022, they informed Jason that he had resigned, stopped paying him, and restricted his access to company documents, finances, and employees. (Yes, you read that correctly. Jason didn't resign. His partners told him that he had resigned. Very fishy.) Jason contacted an attorney to help him seek justice and save his company as well as his intellectual property. The partners, in turn, decided to bring a lawsuit against

Jason, asking the judge to remove Jason from the company and grant them ownership of his intellectual property. He still hasn't found resolution, and the court has not ruled on the case.

Jason's partners were cruel to him and his family. They were dishonest with Jason's employees. And they drove the business into deep debt. Yet when Jason described them and the terrible situation they put him in, he spoke as someone who was trying to love his enemies. He didn't harbor malice in his heart. Instead, he pursued peace. He sought righteousness. He was a living, breathing Beatitude.

His partners prohibited Jason from doing a job he felt called to do. He couldn't design for any new games while in this messy middle between running his company and being completely severed from it. Some days he struggled with overwhelming sadness—completely normal considering the circumstances.

Work-related hurt and the displacements that result can lead us into dark places. We know from the Shepherd's Psalm that God is with us in the valleys, protecting and guiding. But perhaps we forget that the valley can be a place of hope, a place of vision.

LIGHT IN THE VALLEY

The city of Jerusalem was built in the hill country of Judah, about 2,500 feet above sea level, so it could be defended on all sides. Paradoxically, the prophet Isaiah called Jerusalem—the city on a hill—"the valley of vision." Isaiah 22 contains an oracle about Jerusalem. It was a prophecy that hadn't happened yet. Isaiah described the inhabitants of Jerusalem going up on their rooftops to look at the destruction. They take it all in: A battle has occurred. The leaders have fled. Others have been taken captive. That's precisely what happened when Jerusalem fell. Nebuchadnezzar's army laid siege to the city and ultimately burned it to the ground. Zedekiah, king of Judah, and his soldiers ran away. And many people of Judah went into exile in Babylon.

The words of Isaiah 22 were a promise—a promise of judgment. The Lord would level Jerusalem if the people of Judah didn't change their ways. Isaiah prophesied,

> The Lord, the LORD Almighty, has a day
>   of tumult and trampling and terror
>   in the Valley of Vision,
> a day of battering down walls
>   and of crying out to the mountains. (Isaiah 22:5)

But not all would be lost. Along with his words of warning, God gave his people hope. He would do a new work in Jerusalem, that city on a hill. The city would once again be a place of prosperity and peace. God's people would praise him singing, "We have a strong city; God makes salvation its walls and ramparts" (Isaiah 26:1).

Work-related hurt can make us feel like an exile. It can cause vocational, relational, and spiritual displacement. When work beats us up and we tumble into a deep, dark valley, we need light. We need hope. We can move toward others and move toward God in the midst of moments of separation and loss. We can grieve and lament. But what's next? How do we begin to find our way forward?

DISCERNING GOD'S VOICE IN OUR DISPLACEMENTS

Henri M. Nouwen and his friends Donald P. McNeill and Douglas A. Morrison remind us that it's easy to get bogged down by our displacements, but they suggest that our displacements can become places of discernment. Instead of giving into the temptation to bitterness and resentment, they challenge us, "Our first and often most difficult task, therefore, is to allow these actual displacements to become places where we can hear God's call."[1] *Discernment* is the process of recognizing or perceiving. It is a careful and wise quest. When we're talking about discerning God's call, we're talking about *vocational discernment*—the process of paying attention, or perceiving God's invitation to use the gifts and resources he's given us to partner in his redemptive work in the world.

The Quakers have long believed that discernment begins with listening to our lives. Parker Palmer explores this idea in his book *Let Your Life Speak: Listening for the Voice of Vocation*. He writes,

> Vocation does not come from willfulness. It comes from listening. I must listen to my life and try to understand what it is truly about—quite apart from what I would like it to be about—or my life will never represent anything real in the world, no matter how earnest my intentions.... Vocation does not mean a goal that I pursue. It means a calling that I hear. Before I can tell my life what I want to do with it, I must listen to my life telling me who I am. I must listen for the truths and values at the heart of my own identity, not the standards by which I *must* live—but the standards by which I cannot help but live if I am living my own life.[2]

It may seem counterintuitive, even un-Christian, to begin with listening to our lives. But underneath this wisdom is the assumption that God created us in his image, giving each of us a unique sense of self and purpose.

If we're going to listen to our lives, it's best to do that while we're actually living. When work beats us up, burns us out, and breaks our hearts, the temptation can be to pull the covers over our heads and wait for something better to fall in our laps. But, as we'll see in the story of the Israelites, there's another way: everyday faithfulness. It's taking slow, small, intentional steps—the way we do when letting our eyes adjust to darkness.

> *Vocation does not mean a goal that I pursue. It means a calling that I hear.*
>
> PARKER PALMER

EVERYDAY FAITHFULNESS IN EXILE

When we last encountered the exiles, they were in Babylon trying to deal with their grief and figure out how to be the people of God in a foreign land. The exiles actually arrived in Babylon in waves. The first happened in 605 BC as Nebuchadnezzar came to power. He began a campaign to expand his territory, and Judah was on the list of kingdoms to conquer. In 597 BC, Nebuchadnezzar invaded Judah and took thousands more people into captivity. Nebuchadnezzar's army laid siege to Jerusalem a decade later in 587 BC, destroying the temple and burning the city to the ground. The siege ended in 586 BC, and the final wave of exiles were carried off to Babylon.

Scholars estimate that the total number of people exiled to Babylon was around seventy thousand.[3] That's quite a lot of displaced people. Some of them had been taken from their homes without much warning. Others had suffered Babylonian invasion. And still more had seen their beloved city reduced to rubble. For these exiles, Babylon had the potential to become like a deep, dark valley.

Deep, dark valleys can be uncomfortable. When we're in them, we welcome any indication of relief or rescue. We long for a word of assurance, that everything will be okay. But sometimes we have to wait. God said the Israelites would be in captivity for seventy years (Jeremiah 25:12). He had promised to bring them home and rebuild and restore what Nebuchadnezzar's army had ruined. Since they would be in Babylon a while, God's people had to learn to hear his voice and live their lives in a foreign land. God showed them how in a letter that he sent to the exiles through the prophet Jeremiah.

Remember, the prophet Jeremiah didn't go into exile in Babylon. He stayed behind in Jerusalem and wept amid the rubble. However, in 594 BC he sent a letter to the exiles who were already in Babylon because God had a word for them. Here's how the letter begins:

> This is what the LORD Almighty, the God of Israel, says to all those I carried into exile from Jerusalem to Babylon: "Build houses and settle down; plant gardens and eat what they produce. Marry and have sons and daughters; find wives for your sons and give your daughters in marriage, so that they too may have sons and daughters. Increase in number there; do not decrease. Also, seek the peace and prosperity of the city to which I have carried you into exile. Pray to the LORD for it, because if it prospers, you too will prosper." (Jeremiah 29:4-7)

The letter was essentially a how-to guide for living in exile, and it contained both hope and a stern warning. Let's break down this section of the letter verse by verse.

Build houses and settle down; plant gardens and eat what they produce. God wanted the exiles to know that this would not be a temporary displacement. Tents and takeout wouldn't do. They needed to take steps to create a new life in Babylon. I've never built a house before, but I've planted a garden. It takes effort. And it takes a while to go from unplowed earth to consumable fruits, vegetables, and grains. Even if you wanted to live on speedy arugula alone, you'd have to wait over three weeks from sowing the seeds to harvest. But we can't live on arugula alone. It could take months to have a bountiful harvest and continued sowing, reaping, and tilling to ensure they had enough food to last the entire year. God wanted the Israelites to build the infrastructure for a fresh start. They had to start with the basics—food and shelter. Everyday faithfulness was the way forward.

Marry and have sons and daughters. . . . Increase in number there; do not decrease. The previous verse challenged the exiles to get comfortable long enough to build a house and grow a garden. This one seems to stretch the time horizon even further. Build a house; plant a garden; grow your family. The next generation would be born and grow up in Babylon.

The words at the end of this verse remind me of two other pivotal points in Israel's history. The first was when God made the heavens and the earth. He formed and filled a wonderful world, creating human beings on the sixth day and giving them a very important task scholars have called the cultural mandate. We find it in Genesis 1:28: "God blessed [the man and the woman] and said to them, 'Be fruitful and increase in number; fill the earth and subdue it. Rule over the fish in the sea and the birds in the sky and over every living creature that moves on the ground.'" The "increase in number" part sounds similar to what God told the exiles in Babylon. He encouraged them to be faithful to the command he's given to all people since the beginning of time: *Build families, live in community, and together exercise loving stewardship over all that God has entrusted to your care. Multiply image bearers in Babylon the same way you have done since the beginning of time.*

The second point in Israel's history is when the Israelites were in Egypt. At the end of Genesis, we learn about a severe famine that forced many people—including Jacob and his sons—to flee the Promised Land in search of food. Joseph, one of Jacob's sons, was already there. Joseph's ten older brothers didn't like him very much. So they faked his death and sold him to slave traders. Eventually Joseph ended up in Egypt, won Pharaoh's favor, and landed a position in the government.

Fast-forward about four hundred years, and there's a new Pharaoh in charge. Exodus 1:6-7 tells us, "Now Joseph and all his brothers and all the generations died, but the Israelites were exceedingly fruitful; they multiplied greatly, increased in numbers and became so numerous that the land was filled with them." We don't know much about life in Egypt between what we read at the end of Genesis and the opening verses of Exodus. But based on the evidence, it seems that God's people lived out the cultural mandate in a foreign land.

That faithfulness to God's age-old command to be fruitful and multiply was not all sunshine and roses for the Israelites living in Egypt. When the new Pharaoh came to power, he feared the masses of Israelites and subjected them to brutal oppression, harsh labor, and infanticide. And yet all the while, God built a people for himself—one that he would deliver from Egypt and carry into the Promised Land—a people that would be his treasured possession, his light to the nations.

In the midst of their displacement—both in Egypt and in Babylon—God's people could remain committed to an ancient command. They didn't know what would come of it. Those in Egypt didn't know it would lead to their enslavement. But I bet they couldn't imagine that God would save them from the hands of Pharaoh and lead them to a land flowing with milk and honey. Fruitfulness isn't always about having children. Sometimes it's about doing good work that serves God and others. It's also wise to remember, though, that faithfulness to God does not mean automatic freedom from pain and suffering. But our everyday faithfulness to God can be precisely the place where God shows us his power and presence.

Seek the peace and prosperity of the city to which I have carried you into exile. Pray to the Lord for it, because if it prospers, you too will prosper. Here God gave the Israelites another command, but this one is truly countercultural. He challenged them to love their enemies when they had every reason to hate them. I wonder if some of the Israelites wanted to burn Babylon to the ground in retaliation for what they did to Jerusalem. Some of them wanted to smash Babylonian babies against rocks. Yet God wanted them to do the exact opposite. He told them to build up Babylon and to help it prosper. Seeking the peace and prosperity of Babylon could not be a passive activity. The people of God couldn't sit back and wish for it. They had to work for it.

God wanted the exiles in Babylon to work for the common good. For Steve Garber, to care about the common good is "to see ourselves implicated in history, to see that we share a common vocation to care not only for our own flourishing, but for the flourishing of the world."[4] Miroslav Volf likewise connects the common good with flourishing:

> When it comes to life in the world, to follow Christ means to care for others (as well as for oneself) and work toward their flourishing, so that life would go well for all and so that all would learn how to lead their lives well. . . . A vision of human flourishing and the common good is the main thing the Christian faith brings into the public debate.[5]

To work for the common good doesn't mean we work for the flourishing of only ourselves and those like us. We work for the flourishing of the whole world. When Christ returns, God's shalom will extend "far as the curse is found."[6] And that's precisely how far our efforts should extend in bringing tastes of God's kingdom. Through our everyday faithfulness, we can bring beauty, justice, goodness, peace, truth, and righteousness wherever we are, even in exile, even in the darkest valleys.

Jeremiah's letter also reminds us that, as we work for the common good, we are not alone. God works with us by the power of the Spirit. That's why God tells the Israelites to pray for Babylon as well. Even while the Israelites grieved and lamented what their captors had done, God invited them to intercede for them. Their hearts had to wish for the well-being of their captors. And their hands had to work for it.

Finally, God links his people's prosperity to the flourishing of Babylon. One way to think about this is with the saying "A rising tide lifts all boats." If Babylon was flourishing economically, socially, and spiritually, it's likely that God's people who lived within Babylon would flourish as well. Flourishing in moments of displacement is possible. Everyday faithfulness is key. When Jason got kicked out of his business, he committed himself to everyday faithfulness—the

> *Flourishing in moments of displacement is possible. Everyday faithfulness is key.*

work of caring for his two small children and doing small construction projects for his church. He also found new ways to apply his creativity and design skills through painting.

For those of us who have faced work hurt and are wondering what to do next, God's word to the exiles and Jason's story remind us that the next thing is to keep on living. A modern letter to us in our moments of displacement, when we're deep in the valley, might be this: "Wake up, get out of bed, love God, and love your neighbor. Do good work—whether in your current job, your next job, or while you're spending time with family and friends." That's everyday faithfulness.

BE CAREFUL WHAT YOU HEAR

Everyday faithfulness is like taking slow, intentional steps when we're letting our eyes adjust to the darkness. My extended family takes a weeklong beach vacation every summer. One year my bedroom had a four-poster bed. I recall one night getting up, going to the bathroom, and drearily rushing back to bed. But I didn't make it. I smacked my head on one of the posts. Wham! I hadn't given my eyes time to see in the dark and nearly ended up with a minor concussion.

When we're surrounded by darkness, the pupils in our eyes get bigger to allow in even the tiniest bit of light. What was once obscured becomes faintly visible, enough that we can carefully make our way forward. Work hurt can cast us into the shadows of the darkest of valleys. Everyday faithfulness gives us the time and space for our eyes to adjust to the dark. It creates the environment for the valley to become the place of vision.

The final part of Jeremiah's letter reminds us that we can make grave mistakes when we feel like we're in the dark. This section of

Learning to See in the Dark

the letter often gets ignored, but it merits our attention because it contains a stern warning. God told the Israelites, "Do not let the prophets and diviners among you deceive you. Do not listen to the dreams you encourage them to have. They are prophesying lies to you in my name. I have not sent them" (Jeremiah 29:8-9). He warned them not to follow the wrong light.

Before the exile, Jeremiah had prophesied that Judah would fall to Babylon and that Judah's King Zedekiah would serve Nebuchadnezzar (Jeremiah 27). The exile would last for seventy years. God also warned his people not to listen to the words of prophets who would tell the exiles what their itching ears longed to hear—a word of hope that they'd be returning to their land sooner than God had said.

Along came Hananiah. He proclaimed that the exile wouldn't be that long after all. He prophesied that in two years—not seventy—God would break the yoke of Babylon, return the temple articles Nebuchadnezzar stole, and bring the exiles back home. I'm sure those words ushered in relief for the people who had been displaced from all they held dear . . . relief until God struck fear in their hearts. God spoke through Jeremiah, "Listen, Hananiah! The Lord has not sent you, yet you have persuaded this nation to trust in lies. Therefore this is what the Lord says: 'I am about to remove you from the face of the earth. This very year you are going to die, because you have preached rebellion against the Lord'" (Jeremiah 28:15-16). Two months later, Hananiah died.

Jeremiah's letter was a reality check for the people in exile. They would be in Babylon for seventy years (Jeremiah 29:10). There would be no shortcuts. I don't know if they did the math in that moment, but seventy years is a lifetime. Many of them would die in exile, never to return home to Jerusalem. That seems reason enough to despair. And yet God asked them to listen to his voice and rely on his faithfulness as they stared down a long season of displacement. This is where we find everyone's favorite verse: "'For I know the plans I have for you,' declares the LORD, 'plans to prosper you and not to harm you, plans to give you a hope and a future'" (Jeremiah 29:11). God promised to bring them back (Jeremiah 29:14).

But the letter doesn't end on a message of hope. It ends with a stern warning: be careful who you're listening to. The king and the prophets who are with you in Babylon? Ignore them. "'For they have not listened to my words,' declares the Lord, 'Words that I sent them again and again by my servants the prophets. And you exiles have not listened either,' declares the Lord" (Jeremiah 29:19). What a scathing indictment.

In moments of displacement, we can be tempted to listen to any promising word. It reminds me of the scene in Pixar's *Finding Nemo* when Marlin and Dory are searching for Nemo in the deep, dark ocean. Dory, desperate for a sign of hope, sees a light and swims toward it only to discover it's not a real light but the lure of a hungry anglerfish. She's nearly eaten alive. We face similar peril when we're in our darkest moments. We can be easily allured by sweet-sounding words of hope.

An old saying goes, "If it sounds too good to be true, it probably is." The Israelites needed this wisdom. We can heed it today. Discernment is a careful and wise quest, and we have to practice it when trying to perceive God's invitation to us in any given circumstance. First, we have to know God's voice—not necessarily the audible sound, but the consistency and character of how God expresses himself. God's voice reverberates in tones that sound like life in the kingdom. It resonates with virtues like love, hope, mercy, justice, compassion, redemption,

> *Discernment is a careful and wise quest, and we have to practice it when trying to perceive God's invitation to us in any given circumstance.*

and reconciliation. We come to know God's voice through the Scriptures, especially the works and words of Jesus. I think of the Berean Christians in Acts 17. Paul and Silas preached the gospel in their synagogue, and the Bereans went into discernment mode. They liked what they heard "and examined the Scriptures every day to see if what Paul said was true" (Acts 17:11). They were confirming that what they heard with their ears was consistent with what God had revealed in his Word.

We also come to know God's voice through paying attention to what we perceive in our spirits. The apostle Paul suggests that the Holy Spirit communicates with our spirits in a special way (Romans 8:16). My spiritual director describes this as our inner witness. Maybe it's a voice. Maybe it's a stirring in our heart. What, deep down inside, do you know to be true? As best as you can discern, what do you sense to be God's invitation in this moment?

Finally, discernment needs to be done in community. We need one another to confirm or confront what we think we're perceiving. And we need others to hold us accountable and keep us aligned with the character of God and the values of the kingdom. For some discernment processes, the Quakers use clearness committees to help an individual draw on the wisdom of others as they attend to their inner witness. Parker Palmer writes that the clearness committee begins with the assumption that "each of us has an inner teacher, a voice of truth, that offers the guidance and power we need to deal with our problems" and the reality that we live in a loud world makes listening to our inner witness difficult.[7] I've personally never convened a clearness committee, but I have reached out to several trusted friends and advisers in seasons of discernment. They have asked good questions about my situation, my pain points, and my hopes. And they've been able to affirm my gifts and strengths while at the same time being unafraid to challenge me. We learn from this practice that wise questions, asked in community, can help us hear more clearly.

To practice discernment, we have to realize that God is not absent from us in the moments of displacement. We don't need some special spiritual practices or solitude retreats to receive encouragement and a fresh vision from God. We can practice discernment right where God has us, even if it's a deep, dark valley. We don't need a mountaintop moment to hear God in the midst of displacement because God is present with us wherever we are (Psalm 139:7-12). Our job is to learn to hear God's voice when we're in those dark moments—to welcome the valley as a place of vision. And sometimes that call can be as simple as an invitation to everyday faithfulness.

Arthur Bennett, a twentieth-century English pastor, curated a selection of Puritan prayers. He introduced them with a prayer of his own, which also became the title of the collection. Bennett's prayer "The Valley of Vision" captures both the reality of darkness and possibility of light when you find yourself at the bottom. It contains this plea:

> Let me learn by paradox
> that the way down is the way up,
> that to be low is to be high,
> that the broken heart is the healed heart,
> that the contrite spirit is the rejoicing spirit,
> that the repenting soul is the victorious soul,
> that to have nothing is to possess all,
> that to bear the cross is to wear the crown,
> that to give is to receive,
> that the valley is the place of vision.[8]

The prayer concludes with asking God to let the petitioner see light in the darkness and glory in the valley. That's precisely what we want when work has beaten us up, burned us out, and broken our hearts, isn't it? We need God's light to shine into and overcome the darkness. We yearn for that valley to be a place of vision. For new life to spring out of death. Here's the good news: it can. But sometimes we're in the valley for a while—maybe even a long while. It's then, when the light grows dim, that we need to learn to see in the dark.

NEW HOPE FOR LORA

Day after day, Lora, the brilliant educator who started Joy Village School, went to work in her dark basement-level office at a job she didn't really enjoy. Over time, she paid off most of the loans she took out to keep Joy Village afloat. She wrestled with the Lord and tried to discern what God had next for her. Lora practiced everyday faithfulness when she had no other options.

Then, in the two-week period between when we set up our interview and I met Lora in her office, something happened—well, two somethings, actually. First, Georgia's governor Brian Kemp signed into law The Promise Scholarship Act, which "will provide $6,500 per student to families zoned for public schools in the lowest performing 25 percent of the state, to send the student to a private school."[9] Normally, Lora would oppose this sort of legislation, but some friends helped her to see that this law could actually give families in her area money to help cover tuition at Joy Village School. Second, one of the granting agencies Lora had contacted the previous year invited her to apply for a funding opportunity that would not only help her restart the school but also pay her salary for a year while she planned and prepared. She told me, "I had just surrendered this dream and had started reaching for other dreams." In the middle of the valley, she had continued to discern God's calling and listen to his voice. While she committed to everyday faithfulness and did the work that was right in front of her, it seemed God had been on the move through the state legislature, a funding organization, and in Lora's heart.

WORK HURT CLINIC

Symptoms: Have you experienced any of the following in the wake of work hurt?
- Sadness
- Hopelessness
- Despair

Assessment:
- How deep did the valley feel?
- How dark was the valley?
- To what extent did your sadness, hopelessness, or despair affect you, those around you, and your daily activities?

Care:
- Make a plan to practice everyday faithfulness.
- Look for light.
- Attune yourself to God's voice.
- Pay attention to your spirit.
- Lean into community.

4

Sensing a New Calling

"I'M JUST NOT SURE WHAT GOD WANTS ME TO DO." Beth felt stuck. She was trying to figure out what to do following five years of frustrating small business ownership. She and her family had some major expenses on the horizon—college tuition and car payments. They needed her to earn more money, but her business wasn't generating the revenue she had hoped.

In 2018, Beth sensed God calling her to start a business. She had long dreamed of designing and selling greeting cards. She didn't have much money to invest in the business at first but had enough to start a shop on Etsy. Sales were slim. When God provided her a small financial gift through the generosity of some family members, she used the money to make prints and postcards that she could sell at craft shows. But the Covid-19 pandemic derailed that plan.

So Beth pivoted to creating an online website to sell prints and postcards. She was also accepted into a local small business accelerator program that provided her coaching, funding, and access to legal services to help her grow her online store. She received a big boost from that program: her assigned business development coach advised her to apply for a Covid grant. That grant turned out to be the seed money she needed to finally print and sell the cards she had yearned to make.

Starting a business is difficult, and Beth admitted to making mistakes along the way. But starting a business that never makes money can be devastating. It's one of the many types of work hurt that can cause all sorts of displacements in our lives. For Beth, her disappointment led her into a season of vocational displacement. She had lost her sense of calling and was wondering when God would help her find it. She was praying, reading her Bible, writing in her journal, and seeking counsel from friends. In the midst of her vocational displacement, she was engaging in vocational discernment.

UNDERSTANDING VOCATIONAL DISCERNMENT

To engage in vocational discernment is to attempt to perceive or gain clarity about your vocation, or calling. The English word *vocation* comes from the Latin *vocare* meaning "to call." In the Old Testament, the Hebrew word often translated "to call" is the verb *qara*. The New Testament writers primarily used two word families stemming from the Greek verbs *kaleō* and *phoneō*. These words had similar usage and meanings, but *phoneō* was the one that often implied an audible sound or tone. When we study the use of these words throughout Scripture, we can get a sense of what it means to call someone or to have a calling.

First, to call someone or something is to name or label it: "You are to call him Jesus" (Luke 1:31) or "island called Patmos" (Revelation 1:9 ESV). Second, to call someone is to summon or gather them in close: "The LORD . . . called Moses to the top of the mountain" (Exodus 19:20) or "Jesus called the crowd to him" (Matthew 15:10).

The Hebrew verb *qara* appears over seven hundred times in the Old Testament. God is the caller in only a handful of those occurrences. The New Testament writers, especially Paul, often used forms of *kaleō* and *phoneō* to talk about the Christian's call to belong to Christ. In these instances, God is the caller. God calls us

Sensing a New Calling

into salvation, to life in God's kingdom, and to eternal life. We are called by God's grace and to a particular way of life that is consistent with the values of the kingdom.

In Scripture, we see God ask some people to do very specific tasks and take on special roles: Abraham, Moses, Samuel, David, Isaiah, Jeremiah, Mary, the twelve disciples, and the apostle Paul. A form of the word *call* is in the story of Samuel and in the Gospels when Jesus summons the twelve disciples. Hebrews describes Moses' brother Aaron and Abraham as being called. And Paul refers to himself as called. But statistically, these folks are in the stark minority. When we compare those God called to a specific task to all of the people alluded to or referenced in the Bible, we're talking a few grains of sand on a vast seashore. And the stories of those who received specific callings are so different it can be difficult to make sense of them and form some sort of model for vocational discernment. Susan Maros suggests that we want a biblical model of calling—and I would add vocational discernment—because we're "often unconsciously asking for certainty and security. We perceive uncertainty to be antithetical to faith. We want to *know* our calling, to feel safe and secure that God is in charge and at work, that our lives have purpose and meaning."[1] So what can we learn from these stories?

A careful examination of several of the instances in which God called individuals or groups shows that God summons and then gives them something to steward for his purposes. In Exodus, God called Bezalel and "filled him with the Spirit of God, with wisdom, with understanding, with knowledge and with all kinds of skills" to make beautifully crafted adornments for the tabernacle (Exodus 31:1-3). Jesus called his disciples to himself and gave them power and authority to accomplish his mission. Jesus also summoned people and healed them so they could bear witness to God's redemptive work (Mark 10:49; Luke 13:12).

A couple of Jesus' parables—both of which contain the verb *kaleō*—are particularly instructive for us because they describe what life with God would look like between Jesus' ascension and return. The parable of the talents begins with describing a man "who called his servants and entrusted his wealth to them" (Matthew 25:14). The parable teaches us that Jesus gives his followers resources, each according to our ability, that we are to steward well. Like the person given five bags of gold, we're to put to work the resources Jesus has given us. We're not supposed to be wicked and lazy like the person who hid his one bag. A similar parable in Luke's Gospel illustrates the same principle. In this telling, the man entrusting his wealth to his subjects commands, "Put this money to work . . . until I come back" (Luke 19:13). These passages also show how we will be called to give an account of what Jesus has entrusted to us. This is why I like to talk about calling as God's invitation to use the gifts and resources he's given us to partner in his redemptive work in the world. It's a natural outworking of responding to the call to follow Christ.

Our vocation and our occupations. The words *vocation* and *occupation* have become synonymous for many people. Someone asks what your vocation is, expecting you to tell them what you do for a living. Steve Garber reminds us that vocation and occupation are not the same, though. "The former," he writes,

> is the longer, deeper story of someone's life, our longings and our choices and our passions that run through life like a deep river; the latter is what we do day by day, the relationships and responsibilities we occupy along the way of our lives, more like the currents in a river that give it visible form.[2]

Garber also reminds us that it's not wrong—in fact it's quite good and holy—to seek coherence between our vocation and our occupations.

Yet many people around the world may never have the opportunity to experience alignment between their work and their sense of calling. Their circumstances constrain their opportunities to use

Sensing a New Calling

the gifts that God has given them in their jobs. Still, God's call to partner in his redemptive work remains, and we can do that by exercising everyday faithfulness no matter where we find ourselves. Even if we are limited in our ability use our gifts, knowledge, and experience in a certain job or season of life, perhaps we can look for small ways and other places to use those gifts. Perhaps we can use them in our church, through volunteer work in our community, or mentoring a younger person. Jesus' observations about the poor widow's offering encourage us to see the beauty in generously giving what we can (Luke 21:1-4).

The process of vocational discernment. Vocational discernment is a process, but it's not a step-by-step process like a recipe. It's not a linear process at all. Instead, it's a bit more like wayfinding.[3] Pacific Islanders have been practicing wayfinding for centuries. Before they had maps and compasses, these explorers used clues in their environment—the position of the sun and stars, the swells of the seas, the movement of the winds and clouds, and the behavior of animals—to help them cross the seas from one place to the next.[4] Wayfinding requires paying attention to what's going on around you; it engages all of your senses—including your intuition. Wayfinding does not yield precise GPS coordinates. Rather, it gives you a bearing, enough information to make your way. The goal of vocational discernment is to get a sense of direction, a bit more information to help us continue on the way of faithfulness. Even if it yields only one more degree of clarity than we had before, engaging in vocational discernment can help us move toward the alignment between vocation and occupation that Steve Garber described.

> *The goal of vocational discernment is to get a sense of direction, a bit more information to help us continue on the way of faithfulness.*

Paying attention to God. We can't discern our calling without knowing what the caller's voice sounds like. Jesus told his disciples, "I am the good shepherd; I know my sheep and my sheep know me" (John 10:14). He goes on to say that his sheep will know his voice; they will heed him when he calls. To hear God's call, we need to comprehend the depth of the Father's love for us, learn what he cares about, grow in what it means to live out the values of his kingdom. We need to practice being obedient to Christ and develop dependence on the Holy Spirit. We won't do any of this perfectly, but we can pay attention to God by trying to abide in Christ and drawing from him as the branches draw life from the vine (John 15:1).

Paying attention to our community. Have you ever sensed God calling you to do something, but you weren't sure that you heard clearly or correctly? This is where community can help. By community I mean trusted relationships with people who love us enough to tell us the truth—even the hard truth. These people know us well and have walked with us through highs and lows. They know our gifts and our faults. They see our potential and our blind spots. They're our friends, family, mentors, teachers, spiritual directors, therapists, and perhaps even our bosses. When we sense God calling us to do something, we can ask them to pray with us, ask us clarifying questions, and even challenge us. And we ought to pay attention to what they say because God could be speaking to us through them.

Paying attention to ourselves. God has created us with certain dispositions and given us gifts, experiences, and knowledge to steward well. That means we have to cultivate some level of awareness of who we are and what we have to offer the world. In his book *Courage and Calling: Embracing Your God-Given Potential*, Gordon T. Smith writes, "In discerning vocation, in responding to the call of God on our lives, nothing is so important, nothing is more central than coming to terms with our *selves*."[5]

Paying attention to ourselves certainly involves understanding the gifts, skills, knowledge, and experience God has entrusted to us.

Sensing a New Calling

What are you really good at doing? Figuring out complex problems? Simplifying difficult concepts? Making people feel welcome in a new space? What sort of skills do you have? Rebuilding transmissions? Writing? Calculating the precise amount of steel needed to construct a bridge?

Paying attention also includes noticing what activities give us life. Where do you experience what psychologist Mihaly Csikszentmihalyi called "flow"—where you're so engaged in work that's so enjoyable that you're completely absorbed in it to the point of losing track of everything going on around you, including time? Is it when you're designing a new product? Building macros on a spreadsheet? Talking to someone about their hopes and dreams?

Pastor Brad Bell encourages his listeners to look for a "holy discontent" given to us by God.[6] He says a holy discontent is an issue or problem on our heart that keeps us up at night or wakes us up in the morning. It's a sense that something is wrong in the world and we've got to play a part in fixing it. Do you feel the need to help the families in your community have better access to quality day care? Or do you want to develop a neighborhood using sustainable building and landscaping techniques so that you can better care for the environment? If so, pay attention to that. It's a clue.

Paying attention to the world around us. Frederick Buechner famously wrote, "The kind of work God usually calls you to is the kind of work *(a)* that you need most to do and *(b)* that the world most needs to have done.... The place God calls you to is the place where your deep gladness and the world's deep hunger meet."[7] We can't know what the world most needs without engaging the world. It's tempting to spend our lives on our screens, learning about the world in bite-size snippets. It's also easy to see suffering around us and then ignore it as the priest and Levite did the naked and beaten man they passed on the road from Jerusalem to Jericho (Luke 10:30-32). But we must pay attention. We must listen to the world that groans for redemption (Romans 8:18-23). In the world's cries, even in our suffering, we may discern a calling to be a messenger of hope.

Discernment amid everyday faithfulness. When I was twenty-six, I attended a big Christian leadership event in which a famous pastor told the audience that we needed to have a clear calling from God. He even suggested we might go on a mountaintop retreat to find it. I wish I could tell my younger self that's not how it works. The goal of vocational discernment is direction, not certainty. It's a bearing, not a precise destination, that we're after. And we certainly don't need a mountaintop retreat to find it. Maros recommends, "Perhaps rather than looking to the Bible for a road map, we should see the Christian Scriptures as the testimony of brothers and sisters who, like us, have encountered God in the midst of their ordinary life circumstances."[8]

If we closely examine the stories of those who received specific callings in Scripture, we can see that the calling rarely happened in the context of a silent retreat or mountaintop experience. Rather, those callings often came to people in the midst of their mundane lives. God called Abram to leave Haran and journey to the Promised Land (Genesis 12:1). Yet the Bible tells us nothing about Abram's circumstances. For all we know, he was doing what nomads of the ancient Near East did day in and day out. Yes, God spoke to Moses from a burning bush and called him to return to Egypt to lead God's people out of slavery. But Exodus 3 does not begin with the words, "Now Moses was sitting in the middle of nowhere waiting on a word from the Lord." Instead it begins, "Now Moses was tending the flock of Jethro his father-in-law" (Exodus 3:1). God called Moses while he was being a shepherd.

Samuel was trying to get a good night's sleep (1 Samuel 3:3). Saul was looking for his father's donkey (1 Samuel 9:3). David was tending sheep (1 Samuel 16:11). Peter, James, Andrew, and John were fishing (Matthew 4:18-22). Paul was persecuting the church, like the good Pharisee that he was (Acts 9:1). For most of these individuals, their calling to partner in the mission of God in a new way came while they did their ordinary work. God spoke to them in the midst of their everyday faithfulness. *And* they paid attention. During their captivity in Babylon, God called the exiles to do the very same: practice everyday faithfulness and listen to his voice. I think those two practices prepared God's people to hear when he called them to return home to Jerusalem.

THE CALL TO RETURN HOME

Babylon didn't stay in power forever. God had used Nebuchadnezzar and his mighty nation to exercise judgment on Judah, but God would have his vengeance on Babylon in the end. Isaiah 41 prophesied that God would stir the heart of a new ruler who would come to help God's people. In a later chapter, Isaiah said precisely who this ruler would be:

> I will raise up Cyrus in my righteousness;
> I will make all his ways straight.
> He will build my city
> and set my exiles free
> But not for a price or reward,
> says the LORD Almighty. (Isaiah 45:13)

Cyrus conquered Babylon in 539 BC. In addition to Isaiah, we encounter him in four other Old Testament books: 2 Chronicles, Ezra, Nehemiah, and Daniel. The last chapter of 2 Chronicles describes the fall of Jerusalem and the forty-plus years that came after. What we read in 2 Chronicles 36:22-23 we also find in Ezra 1:1: "In the first year of Cyrus king of Persia, in order to fulfill the word of the LORD spoken by Jeremiah, the LORD moved the heart of Cyrus king of Persia to make a proclamation through his realm and also to put it in writing." The essence of that proclamation was this: God called Cyrus to build a temple in Jerusalem, and any of the people of Judah who wished to return home could go and contribute to the work.

Let's zoom in on the phrase "the LORD moved the heart of Cyrus." In Hebrew, the phrase "moved the heart" is a combination of two words: the verb *ur* meaning to alert or rouse and the noun *ruakh* meaning spirit. A better translation might be what the English Standard Version has—"stirred up the spirit." The same verb *ur* appears in Isaiah 41:2, 25, the verses that prophesied the ruler that God would alert or rouse to conquer Babylon. The Bible records several instances of God raising up other nations and their leaders to act on his behalf. God chose Tiglath-Pileser III of Assyria to exercise judgment on Israel (the northern kingdom) and Nebuchadnezzar of Babylon to exercise his judgment on Judah (the southern kingdom). God chose Cyrus to be the leader who would conquer Babylon and set the exiles free (Isaiah 45:13). But based on the evidence in Scripture, Cyrus was the only one among these rulers to receive God's favor. Only Cyrus had his heart stirred.

Cyrus paid attention to the stirring in his spirit. He responded to it with obedience and released the exiles to return and rebuild. But he wasn't the only one whose heart was stirred. After Cyrus's proclamation, Ezra records that many of the exiles prepared to leave Babylon—"everyone whose heart God had moved" (Ezra 1:5). Here again we see the same word combination—*ur* and *ruach*. These people had detected a stirring in their spirits too.

The book of Isaiah gives us a big picture view of what was happening when God stirred Cyrus's heart. Isaiah 45 records that God summoned [*qara*] Cyrus by name, even though Cyrus didn't acknowledge him (Isaiah 45:4-6). God also said, "I have called him. I will bring him, and he will succeed" (Isaiah 48:15). Cyrus's calling came in the midst of building his kingdom. The people's calling came in the midst of everyday faithfulness in exile. And it didn't come with pomp and circumstance. There were no burning bushes or audible invitations—at least that the Scriptures record. God's call to them came in as something quieter than a

Sensing a New Calling 77

whisper or a "still small voice" (1 Kings 19:12 KJV). It came in the form of a stirred spirit, a moved heart.

HEARING GOD'S CALLING IN SEASONS OF VOCATIONAL DISPLACEMENT

When I started seminary, I didn't have a clear sense of calling like many of my classmates did. I sensed maybe God wanted me to do something in ministry or education. But it was fuzzy at best. In other seasons of life, I've had a better idea about how God might want me to use the gifts and resources he has given me in my family, community, and work. In those moments, that sense of direction has energized me to do my best work. Other times, my sense of calling has felt like it was buried under six feet of the red-orange Georgia clay—nearly impossible to unearth.

Different types of work hurt can cause us to lose even the vaguest sense of calling.[9] First, overwork and burnout can zap the sense of purpose we bring to our jobs. We can't even remember why we get up and go to work. Second, it can be tough to remember our calling when we don't get to see the end product or the impact of our work. For example, when I was a teacher, it was pretty easy for me to maintain my sense of purpose because my purpose sat in my classroom every day trying to learn how to solve equations. But when I'm in more behind-the-scenes roles, remembering the sense of calling I once relied on to motivate me becomes more difficult.

Unhealthy workplaces can also distort our sense of calling. Whether we look at workplace culture through the lens of Quiet Quitting or the Great Resignation, it's clear that many of us work in environments that erode instead of enhance our well-being. When you're working for low pay, reporting to a toxic boss, or clocking more hours than you signed on for, it's easy to lose sight of why you took the job in the first place. Ongoing frustration can also cause us to question our calling or to seek a new one. That's what happened to my friend Beth. Five years of floundering business forced her into a season of trying to discern God's calling anew. One day Beth told me, "I'm trying to figure out if God wants me to get a full-time job and make my business a side hustle or keep the business open and figure out how to license my products." I responded, "What if you start applying for jobs, take the next step toward licensing your products, and then see what God does? Vocational discernment is a process that requires paying attention and practicing everyday faithfulness in what God has right in front of you."

WHEN PETER LOST HIS CALLING

Peter was a fisherman.[10] He spent his days with his brother Andrew, steadying their boat, repairing their nets, and hauling their catch to shore. One day Jesus came along and said, "Follow me." He called them into something new: being fishers of people. Without hesitation, Peter and Andrew dropped their nets on the shore of the Sea of Galilee and followed Jesus. It was like a first day at a new job.

John's Gospel depicts Peter as a disciple set on following Jesus. He was focused, undistracted, and undeterred in his work. When Jesus taught that he was the bread of life, some of his followers deserted him. Not Peter. He stayed and doubled down on his commitment to follow Jesus: "Lord, to whom shall we go? You have the words of eternal life" (John 6:68). Peter knew that Jesus was the Messiah, the Son of God (Matthew 16:16).

We may not think of Jesus and his disciples as people who experienced stress in their work, but they did. They had to contend with demons, Pharisees, and hostile crowds. When Jesus began to predict his death, Peter started to unravel. Jesus explained to his disciples that he would suffer, be killed, and then raised to life (Matthew 16:21). Peter wouldn't have it. He pulled Jesus aside and rebuked him for saying such nonsense (Matthew 16:22). Jesus responded to Peter, "Get behind me, Satan!" (Matthew 16:23). I bet Peter's heart plummeted into his stomach, pulled down by the weight of his shame and embarrassment.

Sensing a New Calling

Once Jesus and the disciples arrived in Jerusalem, Peter had to contend with more talk about Jesus' impending death. The night of the Passover Feast, events took a turn. Peter was confused when Jesus got up from the table and washed his disciples' feet in a beautiful act of love and service. The mood was weird and wonderful. But it got weird again when Jesus suggested that one among them would betray him. Peter seemed a little worried it could be him, but he was relieved when Jesus indicated it would be Judas. Peter even reaffirmed his commitment to follow Jesus: "Lord, I am ready to go with you to prison and to death" (Luke 22:33). He would be faithful to his calling, but Jesus wasn't so sure. Jesus told Peter, "Before the rooster crows today, you will deny three times that you know me" (Luke 22:34). Peter said, "Nuh-uh. No way. Not me." The disciples joined him in affirming their allegiance to Jesus. Inside, though, Peter's heart began to turn to stone and crumble.

When the soldiers arrested Jesus in the garden, Peter lashed out. He drew his sword on the high priest's servant, cutting off his right ear. Jesus ordered him: "Put your sword away!" (John 18:11). He'd done it again. He'd disappointed Jesus. Had he acted out of love or fear? Was it exhaustion or grief? Could he trust himself not to deny Jesus?

Peter and another disciple followed Jesus after his arrest. The other disciple went into the high priest's courtyard with Jesus, but Peter had to wait outside in the dark, all alone. Needing the warmth and light of a fire, he joined a few people who had gathered around a small flame. Yet he found no safety with them. A woman recognized him. He had been with Jesus. But Peter denied it. Once. Twice. Three times. When the rooster crowed, Peter realized what he had done, and he wept. He had failed Jesus, and he was overwhelmed with shame. I wonder if Peter also felt incredibly lost—like he had lost his calling.

When Jesus died, I bet Peter thought his calling had died too. How could he fish for people without Jesus there to guide him? Had their mission been buried in the tomb as well? But Peter's calling hadn't died. It had only been buried under stress, shame, and grief. After Jesus rose from the dead, so did Peter's sense of purpose. That resurrection began when Peter ran his fingers over the strips of linen and empty burial cloth. When Jesus appeared to him and the other disciples, commissioning them to go as the Father had sent him, Peter's calling started to come into focus once again. But he didn't have quite enough direction for what to do next, so he returned to the work he knew and loved, fishing.

Early in the morning, after a night without a catch, Peter encountered the risen Lord on the shore of the Sea of Galilee, the place where they first met, where Jesus first called Peter. Jesus challenged Peter, "Let down your nets one more time." Weary but willing, Peter and the other disciples did what Jesus said. To their surprise, they caught loads of fish. After they brought their nets ashore, they had breakfast with Jesus. In that moment, Jesus didn't chide Peter. He didn't rebuke him for denying him three times. Instead, three times Jesus asked Peter, "Do you love me?" and told Peter, "Feed my lambs.... Take care of my sheep.... Feed my sheep" (John 21:13-17). Then Jesus said the words that he first used to call Peter: "Follow me."

WHAT TO DO WHEN WE'VE LOST OUR SENSE OF CALLING

Follow me. It's incredibly simple because it's two words. It doesn't seem like rocket science. There's no magic formula. No step-by-step process. Just *follow me.*

It's exceedingly difficult because it requires effort, intentionality, and Spirit-guided imagination. We have to think winsomely and creatively about what it looks like to follow Jesus today when our accounts of his life are nearly two thousand years old. Following Jesus requires resilience, patience, and grace. No one has ever done it perfectly, and no one ever will. But we seek forgiveness, ask for help, and try again and again and again.

The wisdom for us in Peter's story—for when we've lost our sense of calling—is to carry the truth and power of the resurrection with us into our work. When our calling feels buried and it seems overwhelming to try to unearth it, we can find hope in the fact that we serve a God who raises the dead. Breathing new life into our sense of calling is certainly in his wheelhouse.

> When our calling feels buried and it seems overwhelming to try to unearth it, we can find hope in the fact that we serve a God who raises the dead.

When we feel unsure about what to do in the absence of a clear sense of calling, we need to remember that we are sent into the world to love people the way Jesus did. That means we look for opportunities to

> proclaim good news to the poor
> . . . to proclaim freedom for prisoners
> and recovery of sight for the blind,
> to set the oppressed free,
> to proclaim the year of the Lord's favor. (Isaiah 61:1-2, quoted by Jesus in Luke 4:18-19)

With the Spirit's help, we make an effort to bring glimpses of justice, truth, and beauty to the world around us.

Sometimes, the best way to recover our sense of calling is simply to show up to the work that's right in front of us. It's everyday faithfulness all over again. Our regular work is likely the last place we had our sense of calling. Maybe we start there as a way of retracing our steps. Maybe we can find a way to listen to our life and return to what we can do well. We can do good work and see what God has in store for us. Peter retraced his steps. He went back to fishing.

And that's where he encountered Jesus and found his calling once again. Perhaps, like Peter, in the midst of our everyday and sometimes very ordinary work, we will hear the voice of Jesus calling us anew: *follow me.*

JUST GO

Peter obeyed Jesus' call. So did Cyrus and the Israelites whose hearts God stirred. Will we obey when we sense a new calling from God?

When I lost my job and collapsed to the floor crying, I had to figure out what to do next. I was supposed to drive to Chicago for my PhD program orientation the next day. But why should I when I wouldn't have enough money to pay for more than one class? Was God telling me he didn't want me to get a PhD after all? I was falling down the deep hole of vocational displacement.

After I got off the floor, I finally moved to the couch and sat next to my husband, who had come home from work to comfort me. I told him I didn't know what to do. He said, "Just go and see." So I did. In that moment of displacement, I think that was God's call to me. It didn't come in a burning bush or flash of light. It came in the gentle voice of someone who loved me.

Sometimes everyday faithfulness looks like getting off the floor and moving to the couch, putting one foot in front of the other, or driving one more mile 220 times because you're committed to doing what God has put right in front of you, even if it's difficult, even if you're not sure you're going to hear from him anytime soon. I arrived on campus for orientation shaken and no longer certain of my future. I shared my story with my program adviser, and she said she would see if they had any more scholarship money available. I also met with a former mentor to catch up. I told him my story as well, and he said that he had already planned to offer me a part-time job as his graduate assistant. I think it paid less than ten dollars per hour, but it was good work and a paycheck. Every little bit would help. Those provisions were enough to get me back to campus for my first class, where I felt a strange and unfamiliar stirring in my heart. It was a little bit assurance and a little bit delight. It seemed like a call to keep going, to finish that class and come back for the next one and to pay attention for other invitations that might come my way.

As for Beth, she never got one-hundred-percent clarity about whether she should look for a job or pivot in her business. She told me, "The need for income was pretty strong, and I didn't want to give up on the business that God had me start, but it was starting to seem less practical to be waiting on something that wasn't a sure thing." So Beth decided to keep her business open and apply for jobs. She looked for graphic design and marketing positions. At the same time, she developed a plan for sending card samples to potential buyers. She applied for in person, hybrid, and remote jobs in graphic design and marketing. She had hoped for a part-time role, but most of the openings she saw were full-time positions.

The job-search process frustrated her on multiple occasions. She had to do screening interviews with human resource representatives who couldn't assess her skills or speak confidently about the role for which she was applying. At times she felt ghosted by employers who didn't communicate with her about her application status. And an organization offered her a job at roughly $20,000 below what she had hoped to get as a starting salary.

After evaluating the other benefits the position afforded, such as occasional remote work, a seemingly healthy team, and alignment with the organization's mission, Beth was willing to consider the job. She ended up negotiating a higher salary, and she started her new job a few months after beginning the search. She loves her new job. She and her family quickly saved money to put toward a new car. They purchased dental insurance to cover their child's orthodontic treatments. Immediately she saw the practical benefits of the full-time position.

Six months into the new job, Beth told me,

> I'm really surprised by how much I enjoy being back in the workplace. God knew that. God knew I was going to like it. God knew it would be a place where I could use my gifts. I like being a part of something bigger. I like helping people. I don't have a typical helping profession, but I know that putting my gifts to use is helpful, and that makes me feel good. This organization needed my gifts, and I've made a tremendous impact there in six months. I elevated their visuals with my designs, and people notice the difference on the organization's website.

Even though she never felt like she received one-hundred-percent clarity from God about whether or not to get a full-time job, Beth paid attention and found her way forward with the direction she had. In her case, that direction combined the reality of needing income and the opportunity to serve others using her gifts. Beth practiced everyday faithfulness and paying attention to God throughout every step of the process. And she took courageous steps of faith using the bearings God had given her.

WORK HURT CLINIC

Symptoms: Have you experienced any of the following in the wake of work hurt?
- ▶ Lack of clarity about your calling
- ▶ No sense of calling or purpose
- ▶ Clear sense of calling, but no clear place to exercise it

Causes: Which of the following could have contributed to your symptoms?
- ▶ The confusion between *vocation* and *occupation*
- ▶ Not knowing how to discern your calling
- ▶ Believing you needed to receive a clear calling from God
- ▶ Work hurt

Sensing a New Calling

Care: Practice wayfinding.

- Pay attention to God.
- Pay attention to your community.
- Pay attention to yourself.
- Pay attention to the world.
- Commit to everyday faithfulness.

5

Staying on Task

JOB APPLICATIONS ARE MY NEMESIS. It's not the resumes and cover letters that bother me. It's the rejection. I almost didn't apply for my job at the De Pree Center because I didn't think I could handle another no. Yet sometimes applying for jobs is part of everyday faithfulness. It's a logical and often necessary next step when work breaks our hearts.

During the Great Depression, over 12 million people in the United States were out of work. The unemployment rate—the percentage of people actively looking for work—rose to 25 percent in 1933. People moved throughout the country searching for jobs, desperate to feed their families. The highest unemployment rates since the Great Depression have occurred during my lifetime—nearly 10.8 percent in 1982 and 9.9 percent in 2009 during the Great Recession. In 2023, the global unemployment rate was just over 5 percent. As of 2024, the unemployment rate in the United States was below 4 percent.

Economic changes aren't the only factor driving people to search for new jobs. Gallup reported that millennials, those born between 1980 and 1996, change jobs more often than Gen Xers and Boomers.[1] Gallup suggests two reasons for these changes: millennials earn lower wages compared to previous generations and they're not very engaged in their jobs. Emerging research on Gen Z indicates that they will far outpace all of the previous generations in terms of changing jobs.

Even when unemployment rates are low, many people are still desperate to find a new job—they've lost or left a job and need a new one to keep a roof over their heads, or they need to get out of a toxic situation that's eroding their well-being. Others desire a job that's a better fit for their strengths, experience, and other life commitments. And some just want to earn a paycheck doing something more meaningful. Unfortunately the average job search can take months. It seems like it shouldn't be as tough as it is to find a new job. Stepping into the job market brings the risk of more heartache for already weary workers.

LOOKING FOR A NEW JOB

Greg started working for his college alma mater after graduating. Initially, he loved his job, but then he grew increasingly frustrated by the institutional changes that accompanied a new administration. He observed the culture of the school change into something he barely recognized. His department had endured high turnover, decreased staffing, and shrinking program budgets. In August 2022, he felt at peace about leaving the school. That sense of release motivated him to begin looking for a new job.

After two years of searching, Greg had submitted over fifty applications and even had a few on-campus interviews, indicating that he made it to the final round for a couple of positions. Yet he received only one job offer, which he declined because the opportunity wasn't a good fit for his family. Greg responded well to some of the rejection he faced. He felt unsettled about some of the positions during the hiring process, which made not getting those jobs tolerable. For other positions, he realized that the rejection wasn't about him. The ones that stung the most were the positions he felt great about and yet never heard anything from the potential employer after applying. They ghosted him.

Greg began the search with a positive attitude and a growth mentality. He applied for some "dream roles" that may have been beyond his reach, yet he wondered what he could learn from the application process—not only about the industry but also about himself. At the outset, he had trust and confidence in God that the right job would come. But after months of searching, he began to feel a sense of desperation in his current job, knowing that something needed to change soon. I asked him if, at some point, he might walk away from his job without another offer on the table. He was hopeful that the Lord would provide, but in the waiting, he wanted to do good work where the Lord had him. Yet at the same time, he wondered how long he could be in his role and still serve well. At what point did diminishing returns kick in?

Greg admitted that he could have been at fault for the difficulty of his job search because he sought to make an upward as opposed to a lateral move. Still, the process left him weary. He felt very alone at times and far from God, like God was silent and didn't care about his situation. Deep down he knew that God was present with him and did care about him, but the waiting allowed doubt to creep in. He sought to remove the doubt by recalling the character of God and remembering the presence of God with him in the midst of the waiting.

CHALLENGES IN THE JOB MARKET

It can be daunting to enter the job market, even when there are more available positions than people looking for them. A major source of frustration for many job applicants is the use of heavily automated online application systems. Many companies have begun using these technologies to help manage large numbers of applications efficiently. Some use artificial intelligence embedded in these systems to screen resumes for experience and skills that most closely match the position requirements. We can be rejected by a computer before a human ever sees our materials. If we're lucky, we'll receive an automated response letting us know that they're moving forward with candidates whose experience and skills more closely align with the role.

Researchers from Accenture and Harvard Business School sought to explore why companies struggled to hire good talent while, at the same time, many capable individuals were unemployed or underemployed. They coined the term "hidden workers" to describe those looking for work who were essentially hidden to employers because of their companies' hiring policies and practices.[2] Applicant Tracking Systems (ATS) were part of the problem. The researchers found,

> [ATSs] exclude from consideration viable candidates whose resumes do not match the criteria but who could perform at a high level with training. A large majority (88%) of employers agree, telling us that *qualified high-skills candidates* are vetted out of the process because they do not match the exact criteria established by the job description. That number rose to 94% in the case of middle-skills workers.

It's difficult for applicants to remain hopeful when they're at the mercy of an algorithm.

Another problem job searchers face is discrimination from potential employers. The United States has laws that prevent hiring organizations from discriminating against applicants on the basis of race, color, religion, sex (which includes gender identity, sexual orientation, and pregnancy), national origin, age, disability, or genetic information.[3] Unfortunately those laws don't deter businesses from allowing bias to enter their hiring processes. Two researchers from the University of California, Berkeley, and one researcher from the University of Chicago designed a study to attempt to measure the amount of discrimination taking place.

They created eighty-three thousand fake job applications and submitted them to over one hundred Fortune 500 companies.[4] They randomly assigned the applications either a distinctively White or distinctively Black sounding name and then randomly varied the age, gender, gender identity, sexual orientation, and political leaning on the applications as well. They observed that applicants with distinctively Black names were contacted by employers less than those with distinctively White names. However, this wasn't true across all employers. Some discriminated more than others. The researchers noted that discrimination tended to occur in industries and jobs that were customer-facing. Through their analysis, they were able to identify twenty-three firms that were actively discriminating against distinctively Black sounding names in their hiring processes.

The researchers from UC Berkeley and University of Chicago also observed some gender discrimination in hiring, but it wasn't all against women, and as with racial discrimination, it wasn't across industries. LeanIn.org and McKinsey & Company's 2023 Women in the Workplace report illustrates some of the discrimination women face in various levels of the corporate leadership pipeline.[5] Women make up 48 percent of entry-level positions yet less than 30 percent of senior vice president and C-suite positions. Men hold 52 percent of entry-level positions, 73 percent of senior vice president positions, and 71 percent of C-suite positions. The statistics are particularly grim for women of color, who hold 7 percent or less of top leadership roles.

Gender bias shows up in interesting ways. Researchers from the University of California, San Diego, observed in one of their studies that overqualified female candidates tend to be hired at the same rate as sufficiently qualified men for a given position. Employers assume that the overqualified men might leave the organization quickly looking for better opportunities whereas overqualified women are more likely to stay. Lead researcher Elisabeth L. Campbell summarizes why this bias leads to poor outcomes for both women and their employers:

> This means female employees will be systematically more qualified than men who work in the same roles. Generally speaking, this means women aren't getting the same return-on-investment for their qualifications compared to men and that women are likely to end up with jobs below their qualification level, relative to men. It also suggests firms might not be hiring women for positions that fully utilize their expertise and experience, which isn't good for the firm's performance in the long run.[66]

Bias and discrimination introduce injustice into the job market that can frustrate job seekers and employees alike.

The job search is a vulnerable process that has the potential for pain and disappointment. It can be downright discouraging, and it's easy to stall out or give up. But the story of the exiles encourages us to work diligently at what we sense God calling us to do, even if it's the work of finding a new job.

> *The story of the exiles encourages us to work diligently at what we sense God calling us to do, even if it's the work of finding a new job.*

ENCOURAGEMENT FOR WHEN THE GOING GETS TOUGH

The first wave of exiles returned to Jerusalem because God had stirred their hearts to rebuild the temple. King Cyrus of Persia sent them to do this work, and the people of Persia provided them with "articles of silver and gold, with goods and livestock, and with valuable gifts" as well as freewill offerings to help them finance the building project (Ezra 1:6). When they arrived in Jerusalem, some of the Israelites also contributed financially to the work "according to their ability" (Ezra 2:68-69).

They started work on the altar after taking some time to settle in their towns. Once the altar had been built and regular offerings and sacrifices resumed, the people began working on the temple. They purchased cedar from Lebanon and hired masons and carpenters. Zerubbabel, governor of Judah, and Joshua the priest supervised the work. After the foundation of the temple had been laid, the people celebrated. Well, some celebrated more than others. The Bible tells us that some of the people were happy and others were sad about the new temple. The weeping and rejoicing were indistinguishable, and the noise was so loud it could be "heard far away" (Ezra 3:13).

Why were some weeping while others rejoiced? The prophet Haggai helps us understand. God told Haggai to ask Zerubbabel and Joshua how the new temple compared to the old one with this series of questions: "Who of you is left who saw this house in its former glory? How does it look to you now? Does it not seem to you like nothing?" (Haggai 2:3). The new temple couldn't compare to the one Solomon had built. The first temple had been destroyed by Nebuchadnezzar and his army in 586 BC. Fifty years later, some would still remember what it looked like in all of its splendor. These people wept, realizing that what they had lost could never be restored to what it once was.

Still, the building continued, at least for a bit. Ezra 4 records that the enemies of Judah and the neighboring tribe of Benjamin wanted to help rebuild the temple. But Zerubbabel, Joshua, and the Israelite leaders would not allow them because God had commanded his people to build it. So instead of helping, the neighbors sought to hinder the work. Here's how they did it:

> Then the peoples around them set out to discourage the people of Judah and make them afraid to go on building. They bribed officials to work against them and frustrate their plans

Staying on Task

during the entire reign of Cyrus king of Persia and down to the reign of Darius king of Persia. (Ezra 4:4-5)

Their tactics worked. God's people stopped rebuilding the temple. The work stalled for about fifteen years. God was not happy about that, and so he sent Haggai.

If I could paraphrase Haggai's first words to Zerubbabel and Joshua, I would put it this way: "Does it make sense to you that you're living in posh houses while my house, the temple, is in ruins?" (see Haggai 1:4). Haggai told them to check themselves: "Give careful thought to your ways. You have planted much, but harvested little. You eat, but never have enough. You drink, but never have your fill. You put on clothes, but are not warm. You earn wages only to put them in a purse with holes in it" (Haggai 1:6). They weren't prospering. They weren't satisfied. They weren't flourishing. Instead they were floundering. Why? Because they focused so much on themselves that they neglected to consider God and honor him. So God punished them by withholding dew and causing drought. He afflicted the work of their hands.

Haggai's words got their attention. The people "obeyed the voice of the Lord their God and the message of the prophet Haggai, because the Lord their God had sent him. And the people feared the Lord" (Haggai 1:12). Notice the shift. Their fear of the Lord outweighed their fear of the surrounding people. And God spoke a word to further encourage them: "I am with you" (Haggai 1:13). Then God stirred up the spirit of Zerubbabel, Joshua, and all the people to get back to work. The phrase "stirred up the spirit" is the same we saw in Ezra when God called Cyrus and the people to rebuild the temple. Here God renewed that call to them, reminding them of the work he invited them to do.

God also encouraged them, "'Be strong, all you people of the land,' declares the Lord, 'and work. For I am with you,' declares the Lord Almighty. 'This is what I covenanted with you when you came out of Egypt. And my Spirit remains among you. Do not fear'"

(Haggai 2:4-5). He also told him that he would once again fill the temple with his glory. And even though this temple couldn't compare to the one Solomon built, God promised, "The glory of this present house will be greater than the glory of the former house.... And in this place I will grant peace" (Haggai 2:9). God motivated his people to get to work by reminding them that they played a role in the redemptive work he was doing in the world.

PRESSING ON

We may not have actual enemies trying to thwart our job-search efforts, but poor hiring processes, rejection, negative self-talk, and unhelpful advice from others can derail our efforts. Needing a new job is stressful, and the job-search process can compound the burden we feel—heaping on worry, doubt, and even shame. When we're tempted to stop our search in exasperation, this portion of the return-and-rebuild story offers us encouragement.

Remember your calling. First, the words God spoke through Haggai challenge us to remember our sense of calling. Regardless of how clear that calling is to us, we can be sure that we're called to follow Christ. That means living in alignment with the vision and values of the kingdom of God and considering what it looks like to serve him faithfully given our circumstances. If God has entrusted us with the responsibility of earning in order to care for ourselves and others, we can steward that responsibility well by continuing in our search. New jobs sometimes fall into people's laps, but more often than not, we have to be active participants in the process. The temple wasn't going to build itself. Nor was the wall.

Sometimes we may need to take a job that doesn't align with our sense of calling. This is the lived reality for millions of people around the world who take a job simply to earn a living. There is honor and value in working to provide for ourselves and our families, and we can still follow Christ and practice the values of the kingdom in jobs that don't clearly sync up with our vocation. We may also need to take a job

Staying on Task

that doesn't align with our sense of calling so that we can rest or heal from work hurt we've experienced in the past. This is what Mina wanted after leaving the company she cofounded. She wanted a job in a big corporation where she could hide. There's no shame in that. God can do amazing work in and through her regardless of whether she's in a cubicle or corner office.

> *New jobs sometimes fall into people's laps, but more often than not, we have to be active participants in the process.*

Clarify your calling. Second, a job search can help us clarify our sense of calling. Evaluating job descriptions, tweaking resumes, writing cover letters, and interviewing can be a practice in discernment. These are wonderful opportunities to listen to our lives and pay attention to the stirrings we sense—or don't sense—in our hearts. I recall how God used the experience of writing a cover letter for a job to help crystallize what I believe about the role of social science research, which has become a core part of my career. From that moment, I was able to clearly articulate how it helps us understand God's world and grow in wisdom.

In 2019, I applied for several full-time jobs. I made it to the final round for one of them and was pretty confident the job was mine based on my on-campus interview. The job focused on helping health sciences professors better understand the science of learning so that they could be better teachers. During the interview, I asked if I would be able to do any research as a part of my job. Not likely—at least not on the sorts of questions I was truly interested in. I felt a little deflated on the inside.

A week or so later, my spiritual director asked some questions to help me further discern if the job was a good fit for me, and one of them stuck with me: "Are you telling me that your calling, as far as you can discern it, is to equip people to be disciples of Jesus and that you're considering taking a job in which you'll equip medical school professors how to teach better?" Her question gnawed at me until finally I broke down crying on a walk. I realized that if I took the job, I'd be denying my sense of calling to engage theology and social science research to help others more faithfully follow God. Right then, I decided I would turn down the offer if it came my way. The next day, I got the auto-generated rejection email from human resources. The rejection didn't bother me too much because of what that process of vocational discernment had yielded. When we're feeling discouraged and need help discerning our sense of calling, God can stir our spirits again.

Remember God's presence. Third, Haggai's words remind us of God's presence with us. At key junctures throughout Scripture, God told his people, "I am with you." He spoke those words to Isaac, Jacob, Moses, and Joshua. Through the prophets, God told his people, "Do not be afraid. I am with you." The angel Gabriel told Mary that God was with her. And before he ascended to the Father, Jesus told his followers, "And surely I am with you always, to the very end of the age" (Matthew 28:20). God's presence offers us assurance, even in our most difficult moments. David prayed,

> Even though I walk
> through the darkest valley,
> I will fear no evil,
> for you are with me;
> your rod and your staff,
> they comfort me. (Psalm 23:4)

God is with us every time we tweak our résumé, customize a cover letter, submit an application, and show up for an interview. God's presence with us doesn't remove the difficulties we face. Rather it provides peace that all will be well in the long run, no matter the outcome now.

After she lost her job at the bank, Rachel had a little over one month to find a new full-time job with benefits. Her company kept her on the payroll for six weeks after terminating her, but she didn't want to rely on the small severance they offered for too long. Still

> *God is with us every time we tweak our résumé, customize a cover letter, submit an application, and show up for an interview.*

reeling with grief and shame from being laid off, she had to make a new résumé and start looking for jobs. Her previous employer offered résumé review, and the tips they offered left her in a tizzy. She didn't know where to start making changes, and she hadn't gone through a full hiring process in over twenty years. When I spoke to her, her eyes filled with tears as she said, "God's got this." She believed that God was present with her and holding her amid so much upheaval and heartbreak.

Remember that God is at work. Finally, the promises God spoke through Haggai help us understand that God is at work beyond what we can see—and we have a role to play. God pointed the Israelites to a new future, giving them hope when their spirits were downcast. In the middle of a job search, we may have no idea what God is doing in our lives and in the lives of those we encounter.

When I was up to my eyeballs in applications, I never considered how my experiences on the job market might shape my work at the De Pree Center. I never envisioned myself as a hiring manager, but in my role, I've led the hiring process for four of my direct reports, and I've served on a handful of other hiring committees. That involves developing job descriptions, determining pay ranges, screening applications, and conducting interviews. It feels like a really sacred part of my role because it deals in livelihoods and dreams. Hiring processes require so much emotional labor on the part of the individuals applying and the hiring organizations because the stakes are so high for both. It gives me deep joy to offer someone a position. And I get a pit in my stomach when I have to call someone to tell them they weren't selected. My experiences on the job market have given me compassion in a part of work life that desperately needs it.

SEEING GOD AT WORK

Gina was a high school teacher who had built an amazing arts program in her school and loved working with her students. As she had with her first child, Gina planned to work until she went into labor. Then she would take her maternity leave and return to her job when it was over. But just days before the birth of her second child, the superintendent instead terminated her contract. He had already hired her replacement. Gina was baffled. How could this happen?

In the midst of a painful situation, God was moving. Gina's work hurt prompted her and her husband to respond to a calling they had sensed from God a year before to move across the country and start a new ministry. When Gina lost her job, they didn't have any clear reason to stay in Florida. So they packed up and left for Seattle in search of new jobs, hoping that God would provide enough for their young family and for them to begin their new venture. They found good jobs and started their ministry. Now, two decades later, they are thriving. Recalling her termination, she told me, "If that hadn't happened, I wouldn't be here talking to you today." She would have probably still been teaching high school in Florida, and our paths would have likely never crossed.

The job search may be filled with all sorts of surprises—some of them welcome and others not. We may find ourselves applying for jobs that seem like a far cry from our dream—the senior executive interviewing for a position as a barista, the information systems analyst working for the Geek Squad. Like the Israelites, we may miss what once was and lament the lesser glory of where we find ourselves. We may also find ourselves, like Greg, on a long journey—wondering where God is and if he will ever answer our prayer for a new job. And some of us may sail through the job search, find a wonderful job, and never craft another résumé in our lives. Regardless of how we experience the job market, we learn from the Scriptures that God is with us always, honoring our work of everyday faithfulness and achieving more than we could ever imagine.

WORK HURT CLINIC

Symptoms: Which of the following have you experienced during a job search?

- Frustration
- Rejection
- Doubt
- Insecurity

Care:

- Commit to everyday faithfulness.
- Remember your calling.
- Clarify your calling.
- Remember God's presence.
- Remember that God is at work.

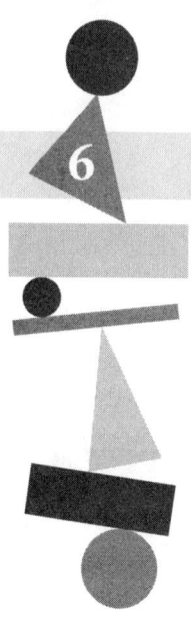

Making Sense of It All

David never set out to become a realtor. He thought he would do it for a few months until the economy rebounded from the Great Recession. After two years, he felt disillusioned from having worked on some unhealthy teams of realtors and having an unsteady income. He was ready to be done, and he was angry at God. He thought he was following God's will when he got his real estate license. Experiencing so much frustration and disappointment simply didn't add up with what he believed to be true about God and work. This sent him into a season of wrestling and discernment.

As a result of his work hurt, David had to engage in *meaning making*—the process of making sense of our experiences and the world around us. It's how we connect the dots. Psychologists who study meaning making suggest that we see the world through the lens of our beliefs, values, goals, and sense of purpose.[1] That means our faith can play a major role in how we interpret what happens to us. When faced with a challenge or stressor, we work to reconcile that situation with what we know to be true. And that's not always easy.

MEANING MAKING IN THE WAKE OF WORK HURT

Meaning making goes by a few different names such as "cognitive reframing" or "getting a new mindset." Shundrawn Thomas, in his book *Discover Joy in Work,* talks about changing your attitude. We can also look at it through the lens of transformative learning. Jack Mezirow, a former professor at Teachers College at Columbia University, is considered the father of transformative learning theory. He believed that one of the fundamental skills we need as adults is the ability to make sense of our experiences and to integrate what we learn from those experiences into our thinking so that they can shape the way we live.

Imagine the way we see and understand the world as a tower of Jenga blocks. That tower has been shaped by our family, culture, language, religion, socioeconomic status, and political commitments. It contains our beliefs and assumptions about the way the world works.[2] We've lived a while, and that's caused us to reconfigure our blocks a time or two. Some of our pieces have been removed from the middle and stacked precariously on the top. The holes are obvious, and the slightest movement makes the whole tower wobble. Along comes a trial or catastrophic event—a difficult conversation, a sobering diagnosis, an unexpected loss—and our tower comes crashing down. Blocks are scattered everywhere. Everything we thought we believed no longer makes sense.

That situation that causes our tower to fall is what Mezirow called a disorienting dilemma. Work hurt—whether it's disappointment, disillusionment, or devastation—definitely fits the bill. In addition to causing us to experience all sorts of displacements, it can be profoundly disorienting. We have a choice when the tower falls down. We can just stand there and look at the blocks chaotically strewn about us, or we can start to pick up the pieces. Transformative learning occurs when we pick up the pieces and examine them before we start reassembling the tower. We look at a particular assumption, belief, or value and ask ourselves, "Why was I holding on to that to begin with? Where did that originate? Do I want to keep it? Or is there a better, more informed way of thinking?"

When work beats us up, burns us out, or breaks our heart, our minds may become flooded with all sorts of negative narratives about our jobs, our bosses, and even ourselves. That's what happened to John. When he asked to see his company's financial statements, he didn't anticipate that to be a problem. John was the business operations manager, after all. Finances fell under his purview. However, the owners of his company didn't want to show him the books. John suspected that they were using business funds for their personal use and wanted to bring transparency and accountability to the company's finances. When the owners resisted and started treating him poorly, a litany of self-critical narratives reverberated in his mind. *I didn't ask the right questions. I did something wrong. Maybe I should have worked harder.*

When the negative narratives take hold, we have to sift through the chaos to figure out what is true, what's healthy, and what's worth holding on to. That requires a healthy dose of critical reflection, which takes time and often the company of other people—whether in person or through other media like books and podcasts. With the help of his therapist, John learned to change those narratives. *I am not my job. I am here to honor and love people, maintain my values, and treat myself with love. I am doing my best.* The outcome of transformative learning is a better, healthier, and, for Christians, a more biblically sound way of looking at the world. We want to build a new tower that's stronger and better constructed than what we had before.

> When the negative narratives take hold, we have to sift through the chaos to figure out what is true, what's healthy, and what's worth holding on to.

In short, our goal is to develop wisdom—to integrate the core lessons we've learned from our experience into our way of being. We can change our thinking about work after it breaks our hearts. But, practically speaking, how do we change the way we think about our work before we encounter the next disorienting dilemma? I'm going to share three strategies: (1) engage in job crafting, (2) think of your work as a calling, and (3) immerse yourself in a bigger story.

ENGAGE IN JOB CRAFTING

In their *Harvard Business Review* article "What Job Crafting Looks Like," Jane E. Dutton and Amy Wrzesniewski define *job crafting* as "changing your job to make it more engaging and meaningful."[3] They break job crafting into three components: task crafting, relational crafting, and cognitive crafting. Task crafting involves reconfiguring your work responsibilities so that you can do what gives life to you at work while still attending to the demands of your job. Some jobs don't allow for this. But if yours does, it might be worth talking with your supervisor about ways you can tinker with your role so that the work feels like a better fit.

Relational crafting requires changing the ways you interact with others at work. Here the focus is people work. Maybe you need to spend less time with a coworker who has a habit of telling crude jokes. Or perhaps you need to schedule weekly collaboration meetings with other creative team members for inspiration. The goal of relational crafting is attending to the places where relational issues are causing strife. Work for reconciliation where you can and remediate what you can't.

Simone engaged in relational crafting to protect herself from her boss's angry tirades. He had started yelling at her frequently during their one-on-one meetings. So she began requesting that they meet in a public space. She assumed he would be less likely to yell at her if they talked in a large open space in their office or at a coffee shop. Her tactics worked.

Finally, cognitive crafting is bringing a new perspective to your work, thinking about its purposes in new ways. It's the work you do following a disorienting dilemma. The next two strategies are forms of cognitive crafting.

THINK OF YOUR WORK AS A CALLING

Bryan Dik and Ryan Duffy are vocational psychologists. Drawing on the research of Amy Wrzesniewski and her colleagues, Dik and Duffy suggest that approaching one's work as a calling can be profoundly beneficial. They write, "For people with a calling, work is far more meaningful than a way to survive and pass the time, or an achievement ladder to climb, it provides an arena for using one's gifts with purpose to the benefit of the common good."[4] They also offer some strategies for learning how to approach your work as a calling: (1) make room for listening; (2) make meaning in your work; and (3) serve others at, in, and through your work.

Dik and Duffy prioritize listening because of how it relates to their definition of calling. They define calling as "a transcendent summons, experienced as originating beyond the self, to approach a particular life role in a manner oriented toward demonstrating or deriving a sense of purpose or meaningfulness that holds other-oriented values and goals as primary sources of motivation."[5] Their definition may come off as secular because they're using language that appeals to a wide variety of people, not just Christians. Listening matters to them because calling is "a transcendent summons," and to hear a summons or receive an invitation, we have to pay attention—to listen. Practically this can involve actively listening for God while engaging in spiritual practices or through reflecting on one's life, one's gifts, and one's capabilities.

Second, Dik and Duffy recommend that we take steps to make meaning in our work. Meaningful work can come as a result of finding a meaningful job, integrating our faith with our work, using our strengths and gifts in our work, framing our work in terms of outcomes that matter, or focusing on who or what our work ultimately serves. In her memoir *Maid: Hard Work, Low Pay, and a Mother's Will to Survive*, Stephanie Land describes how she worked tirelessly as a house cleaner to escape homelessness and build a better life for herself and her daughter, Mia. After a while, working for a cleaning company stopped making sense to her. It didn't align with the type of life she wanted and where she wanted to live. She wrote,

> In wanting that life, in wanting to get ahead, my job at Classic Clean stopped making sense. Over a third of my wages went to gas.... Plus, the anonymity started to wear me down. Between working alone and taking online classes, my life was one of solitude. I craved human interaction, even if it was a situation where I'd been hired by someone to work. I needed my job to have purpose, meaning, or at least feel like I helped someone.

Stephanie quit her job at Classic Clean and began taking steps to go after a life that was meaningful to her—a life that involved moving to the city of her dreams and going to college there.

Third, Dik and Duffy suggest we focus on serving others. "Given the sheer amount of time most people spend working, the workplace seems to be the most consistently available venue for doing something that has beyond-the-self benefit, or for displaying kind, caring, and compassionate behaviors."[6] Arthur C. Brooks, in an article on career advice for *The Atlantic* wrote,

> You are made to love, and your work—no matter what it is—should be the way you express your love. That might sound as if being ambitious or hardworking doesn't matter so long as we have a heart full of love. But that's not the implication. To love others through our work involves bringing our very best effort every day; to be completely, uncompromisingly dedicated to excellence in what we do. Whether we work in a bank, or put roofs on houses, or take care of our children full-time, true love means not cutting corners.[7]

As Christians, we serve others through our work because God has loved us and commanded us to love him and to love our neighbor. When we follow Christ and cooperate with the Holy Spirit in our transformation into Christlikeness, serving others becomes our default way of being in the world. Yet even as we're growing into this way of being, we can practice serving others every day. We can affirm or encourage a colleague, demonstrate kindness to a client, make a way for a customer, or seek justice for a victim. We can buy our coworker a bagel on our way to the office, help our boss with a grant proposal, or open a new checkout line to move customers through the store more quickly. All of these are forms of service that can be done out of love.

This is everyday faithfulness all over again. It's showing up to work with the desire to follow Christ, to love him, and to love others. It's the simplest way we make ourselves available to God to participate in his redemptive mission in the world and in our workplaces.

IMMERSE YOURSELF IN A BIGGER STORY

The third strategy I'm going to offer is that we immerse ourselves in a bigger story—one large enough to hold our work hurt and hope. To illustrate, we're going to focus on Nehemiah 3, the chapter in which Nehemiah describes the work of rebuilding the wall. I love the Bible, but, honestly, there are some parts of Scripture that make my eyes glaze over: genealogies, censuses, and Old Testament laws about skin sores, to name a few. It's difficult for me to engage because it takes time for me to wrap my brain around (a) how these portions of the Bible fit within the larger story and (b) why they're relevant to my life. So it's a small miracle that while reading through Nehemiah a few years ago, I stayed awake through all of chapter three. It's even more of a miracle that what I saw in Nehemiah 3 was the catalyst for what would eventually become this book.

When we last encountered God's people in the book of Ezra, they had just completed work on the temple. This was around

515 BC. Nehemiah was still in Babylon at the time, serving as the cupbearer to the Persian king, Artaxerxes. One of Nehemiah's brothers, along with some friends, traveled from Jerusalem to visit him. Nehemiah recalled,

> I questioned them about the Jewish remnant that had survived the exile, and also about Jerusalem.
>
> They said to me, "Those who survived the exile and are back in the province are in great trouble and disgrace. The wall of Jerusalem is broken down and its gates have been burned with fire." (Nehemiah 1:2-3)

This troubled Nehemiah—moving him to tears. He fasted and prayed. His prayer began with a confession of the sins that he and the Israelites had committed—forsaking God and his commandments. He recalled the consequences of their unfaithfulness and the hope of God gathering the faithful few from "the farthest horizon" to bring them back to Jerusalem (Nehemiah 1:9). Then he asked God for favor in the presence of the king. But the prayer didn't specify why.

In Nehemiah 2 we read that Nehemiah got an audience with the king because, as cupbearer, it was his job to serve the wine. King Artaxerxes noticed Nehemiah's downcast face and inquired why he was so sad. Nehemiah told him about the destruction of Jerusalem. The king asked what Nehemiah wanted. Before responding, Nehemiah prayed again. Then he told the king that he wanted to return to Jerusalem so that he could rebuild it, and the king consented.

Once he got to Jerusalem, Nehemiah set out to survey the damage. He did so under secrecy and cover of darkness. After he had surveyed the damage, he gathered the people he envisioned helping with the work of rebuilding and said to them, "You see the trouble we are in: Jerusalem lies in ruins, and its gates have been burned with fire. Come, let us rebuild the wall of Jerusalem, and we will no longer be in disgrace" (Nehemiah 2:17). The people were willing and ready. The next sentence says, "So they began this good work" (Nehemiah 2:18).

What our English Bibles translate as "good work" is actually the Hebrew noun meaning "the good," "good things," or "goodness." These people had been in exile and returned home to see their beloved Jerusalem still in ruin. They weren't simply moving to a new city where they would buy new homes and find new jobs. No, everything had to be rebuilt from the ground up—the city, its walls, their homes, and their livelihoods. Yet they were able to come together around a shared commitment. God had moved their hearts to return home and rebuild the wall. They believed that the work before them was worthy and good.

In the wake of work hurt, the concept of "good work" can seem downright foreign—even alienating. How can something that has the potential to hurt us so badly actually be good? Many people have a jaded view of work to begin with. I follow a few Instagram accounts filled with memes that communicate that work is inherently bad and something to be escaped. Several posts glorify sleep and the weekend to reinforce just how awful work can be. The possibility of finding good work—work that we enjoy and that may truly be good *to* us and *for* us—seems remote. But good work is out there. Finding good work may be less about landing the perfect job and more about how we approach it. Sometimes we have to change the way we think about our work.

Because I'm a big fan of actually reading the Scriptures, I encourage you to put this book down and read Nehemiah 3—all of it—before you read my summary. This is the part of Nehemiah that describes the rebuilding of the wall around Jerusalem. In our English translation, it's thirty-two verses long, and it's pretty repetitive. The word *repaired* appears thirty-eight times in the NIV translation. The Hebrew words that make up the phrase *next to* appear sixteen times. *Built* or *rebuilt* occur eight times. Pause now to read Nehemiah 3.

Here's the gist of how Nehemiah 3 flows: *Somebody rebuilt one of the gates. Next to him, another guy repaired the adjoining section of wall. Next to him, a neighbor worked on the section from his house to the next gate.* And so on and so forth. When I visualize the scene, I see a big square with dozens of Israelites, brows dripping with sweat in the hot sun, gathered around the wall and doing their work side by side. Those rebuilding the walls and gates weren't just the carpenters, stonecutters, and masons. From Nehemiah 3:1 we can see that the priests—including the high priest Eliashib—were involved. So were some goldsmiths and a perfumer. Other leaders like Shallum of Hallohesh participated in the work, as did his daughters. Temple servants and some merchants worked on the wall as well.

When we look at the story of Nehemiah 3 in isolation, it can be difficult to determine why this passage is in the Bible and what it might be trying to teach us. It would have been much simpler to tag another verse onto the end of Nehemiah 2: "And they rebuilt the wall." But when we look at the flow and details of this chapter in the context of the broader story of God's people returning home from exile, we can discern an important truth that will help us when work breaks our hearts: God calls us to do good work.

The concept of calling is deeply intertwined with God's purposes. In Ephesians, Paul argues that God saved us because he has a purpose for us (Ephesians 2:9-10). Through the prophets, God often revealed his purposes for his people. Moses reminded the people delivered out of Egypt that they were to be an example to the nations in their character and conduct (Deuteronomy 4:6). Jeremiah told the exiles they were to participate in the flourishing of those around them (Jeremiah 29:7). Isaiah said this to the exiles waiting to return to the Promised Land:

> Your people will rebuild the ancient ruins
> and will raise up the age-old foundations;
> you will be called Repairer of Broken Walls,
> Restorer of Streets with Dwellings. (Isaiah 58:12)

Returning home to rebuild the wall was part of God's purposes for his people *at that moment* in history. Yet how God was calling them to participate was for each individual to discern. Some would lead the work. Others would cut the stone and carry it. Still more would repair gates. Each had to understand the good work God had called them to do, but they couldn't think of their calling and their work in isolation.

God calls. The essence of calling is that God invites us to follow him and partner in his redemptive work in the world. Some people discern a call to a particular role or task, and this was the case for those God called to return home to rebuild Jerusalem. In Nehemiah's case, we don't read the words "and God called Nehemiah," or, like we read in Ezra, "Now God stirred the heart of Nehemiah." The Scriptures aren't explicit about Nehemiah's sense of calling, but I think we can infer that Nehemiah discerned a calling to rebuild the wall based on what the Scriptures *do* tell us.

First, Nehemiah had an embodied, emotional response to the news that Jerusalem was in ruins. He sat down, wept, mourned, fasted, and prayed (Nehemiah 1:4). Second, Nehemiah sought God's help in receiving the favor of the king. This implies Nehemiah sensed that he needed to do something; he needed to act. It's not until his conversation with Artaxerxes that we know that Nehemiah wanted to return to Jerusalem to rebuild the city (Nehemiah 2:4-5). Nehemiah knew God's hand was on him (Nehemiah 2:8). It seems Nehemiah sensed a call to oversee this work.

We also need to see Nehemiah's calling in the context of the calling God did in the beginning of Ezra. God stirred the heart of Cyrus. God stirred the individual hearts of the exiles. God invited all of these people to participate in the work of rebuilding. The book of Ezra describes how they rebuilt the temple. Then God called Nehemiah home to lead the work on the wall.

God calls in line with his purposes. God's plans to bring his people home were in motion like a swiftly moving current. Cyrus

Making Sense of It All

heard the call and stepped in the water. Then the Israelites who worked on the temple joined in what God was doing. Finally, Nehemiah and the wall builders surrendered to the flow of God's redemptive Spirit and got caught up in a good work bigger than themselves. That current still flows today. God calls us to step into the river and join in his redemptive work.

God calls us. Second, God calls *us*. Plural. We can't think of our individual callings apart from the callings of every other believer. Susan Maros writes about this in her book *Context and Calling*, noting that many Christians in the West tend to think of calling as something very individualistic. Instead, she suggests, we have to see our individual callings as intertwined with the callings of our communities. Primarily, we have to locate our sense of calling within Jesus' call to the body of Christ: "The community is the context of the calling of individual people. When God appoints someone to a task, it is always with the well-being of the community in mind, and it is always in line with God's broader intentions for the world. And when God appoints an individual, that calling is always in relation to the calling of their community."[8]

Nehemiah knew he couldn't rebuild the wall by himself. That's absurd. He was a cupbearer, not a stonecutter, carpenter, or mason. Plus, the wall was huge. It would take ten lifetimes for him to do the work by himself. That's why he gathered the people "who would be doing the work"

> *When God appoints an individual, that calling is always in relation to the calling of their community.*
> — SUSAN L. MAROS

(Nehemiah 2:16). He had to rally them around the common cause. "Come, let *us* rebuild the wall of Jerusalem, and *we* will no longer be in disgrace" (Nehemiah 2:17, emphasis added). Rebuilding the wall was a group project from the beginning. And the work of rebuilding we read about in Nehemiah 3 proves it. Men and women from all different occupations worked together to repair and rebuild the wall around Jerusalem. God had called them to this work. He had stirred their hearts and led them home. And now they worked together to restore what had been broken. They found themselves—perfumers, goldsmiths, rulers, and priests—side by side putting their city back together brick by brick. When we forget that we're called along with other believers, it's easy to become discouraged. Yet we need to remember that millions of other faithful Christians are alongside us bringing light and truth and hope and peace to a hurting world.

God calls us to good work. Third, God calls his people to good work—to use their thoughts and actions to make a contribution to this world. Even when we can't quite figure out the specifics of what that means for our daily lives and our jobs, we know that we're called to partner in God's redemptive mission. So we can start with the basics of loving God and loving others (Mark 12:28-31) as well as doing justice, loving mercy, and walking humbly with God (Micah 6:8). Anglican priest Tish Harrison Warren reminds us, "Work—whether paid or not, drudgery or a joy, skilled or common—makes a difference. Done well, it adds truth, beauty, and goodness to the world. It pushes back the darkness."[9]

When Jerusalem was reduced to rubble, most of its inhabitants lost their homes and their livelihoods. They were out of work and then jilted out of Judah, carried off into exile in Babylon. When God called them back home, he called them to a common mission—to rebuild the wall. The Bible is relatively silent on when and how they got back to their regular jobs and started participating in any sort of economic activity. The focus in Ezra and Nehemiah is on the work of rebuilding the city—first the temple and then the walls. With the central space of their worship and the security of their city in place, perhaps they could thrive again.

When they returned home from exile, God's people did the work that was right in front of them. It involved cutting stone and stacking bricks. It was the work of everyday faithfulness, but it wasn't glamorous. Sometimes our work situation is so terrible that it's difficult to think of it as an opportunity to serve others. When you're working to survive and keep yourself fed, clothed, and housed, serving others may not seem like much of a priority. Or when you're working in a toxic environment, it can seem overwhelming to muster the energy to love others well when you've been belittled, harassed, or despised. Some jobs may seem completely futile, like they serve no earthly good. Work hurt doesn't make work disappear. Sometimes we wish it would. But the truth is that there is no shortage of opportunities for loving God and serving others with the work of our heads, hearts, and hands. Even the smallest efforts participate in God's redemptive work and can help us make meaning in the midst of challenging situations.

Andy Crouch describes human work as *culture making*. Writing about the work God gave Adam and Eve at the beginning of the world, Crouch says, "They go to work with these recalcitrant raw materials (even the garden before the fall, it seems, required tilling and keeping), forming and reshaping the world they find themselves in. They begin 'making something of the world.'"[10] This is our work today—not merely making things but making sense of them, he argues. That means we can find meaningful work just about everywhere we look. It can be as mundane as doing the laundry or mowing the grass. It can be something we do as a volunteer like serving in a food pantry. It can even be the important inner work of developing our relational skills and growing in self-awareness. All of it is purposeful and all of it can be good work if done for love of God and neighbor.

We have a hurting world in need of the healing hope of the gospel, and we have cities around the globe in need of restoration and repair. When we remember that God invites us to participate in his work to redeem and restore along with all who follow him, we can begin to experience our spiritual, relational, and vocational displacement being set to rights. When we remember that God is at work in and through us to achieve his purposes and can stir our hearts to cooperate with him in his plans (Romans 8:28), we remember our calling. And when we remember that other Christians are colaboring with us to do justice, love mercy, and walk humbly before our God, it strengthens us in our spirit and reminds us we're not alone (Micah 6:8). Focusing on our calling to follow God and participate in his redemptive mission in the world can be radically reorienting and healing. It helps us see ourselves as part of a larger story. It's like when a match comes to light a candle that's just gone out. It brings new light and helps us to see anew.

A DIFFERENT TAKE ON REAL ESTATE

In the midst of wrestling with God about his calling and career, David entered a program that encouraged him to read several books about theology and work. He also learned more about what the Bible teaches about God's redemptive work in the world. David learned where his work fit in God's big story. He could serve others and bring glory to God as a realtor. He framed his work this way: "I can help someone find a place to call home. Having a home allows that person to do whatever work God has allowed them to do in the city, and the city is made all the better as a result." This new perspective on work motivated David to continue in his profession, which he has for over a decade.

If we let the story of rebuilding the wall sink into our hearts and minds, I think it can transform the way we view our work and therefore how we approach it. The key to finding good work is anchoring our work to something bigger than ourselves. We can frame our work as part of God's

> *The key to finding good work is anchoring our work to something bigger than ourselves.*

redemptive mission in the world. And we can find comfort in the fact that we're not alone in it. Around the world, other Christians are trying to pay attention to God and practice everyday faithfulness. In a metaphorical sense, we're standing next to them rebuilding, repairing, and restoring precisely where we are. Brokenness is all around us. We know it's in our work and in our workplaces. And chances are if we've experienced the work hurt, so has someone else on our team or in the same field.

If we can remember that God has called us to a work that's bigger than any of our daily jobs, I think we can get a sense for why our work matters. As I'm working on my part and you're working on your part—loving God and loving others at, in, and through our work—we're engaging with God's redemptive work in the world. We're actively being the city on a hill—or maybe a million beacons of light in the darkness.

WORK HURT CLINIC

Symptoms: Which of the following have you experienced?
- Being unsure what to make of your work hurt
- Questioning what you know or believe about yourself, others, God, or the world of work
- Hearing unhealthy narratives about yourself, others, or God on repeat in your mind

Care:
- Engage in job crafting: task crafting, relational crafting, and cognitive crafting.
- Think of your work as a calling.
- Immerse yourself in the story of God's redemptive work.
- Practice everyday faithfulness.

7

Working in a Battle Zone

AFTER GRADUATING FROM COLLEGE, Brian returned to his hometown to teach elementary school. His community was built around the textile industry and attracted many blue-collar workers, especially migrants. At that time, the number of children receiving free or reduced-price lunch at school was an indicator of the amount of poverty within a school or district in the United States. In Brian's district, all of the children qualified for free lunch.

As a bilingual male with an education degree from a good college, Brian had his pick of elementary school jobs in the district. He chose the school he did because of the principal. He, too, was bilingual and had a philosophy that appealed to Brian: we're going to do the best we can for these kids. Brian loved working for him as well as for the assistant principal during his first year of teaching.

The second year, everything changed. Brian's principal was moved to another school in the district; the assistant principal was replaced as well. When he learned who the new principal was, Brian's jaw dropped. It was a small city, so he knew the man, probably better than most: Brian had dated the new principal's daughter in high school. He was her first boyfriend and had spent time with their family. Unfortunately, their breakup wasn't pretty.

Brian told me that their first interaction in their new principal-teacher relationship was so awkward. From that point on, the principal avoided Brian, even refusing to conduct required observations of his classroom.

The bigger problem was the culture shift in the school. Whereas the previous principal was all about doing the best they could, the new principal was all about test scores. Brian came to dread standardized testing. "I knew I was going to hear it," he told me, meaning he knew the administration would scold him for his children's low scores. This test-driven culture changed how Brian viewed his class. They were no longer children; they were numbers.

Brian taught fourth grade that year. He had twenty-nine students in his class, most of whom spoke Spanish as their first language. Some students had arrived in the United States as unaccompanied minors. One had moved there from Japan and spoke neither English nor Spanish. Half of the students had an individualized education program (IEP). He tried explaining all of this to his assistant principal when she drilled him about his class's low test scores. She replied, "Those sound like excuses." At that moment, Brian thought, *I'm out.* He loved teaching. He loved his students. But this toxic test-score culture was not what he signed up for when he took the job.

TOXIC WORKPLACES

Professor Mindy Shoss wrote, "Toxic workplaces drain all the energy and excitement out of employees and replace it with fear."[1] Brian learned that the hard way. Analyzing data on five hundred companies known for taking strides toward a healthy corporate culture, another group of researchers discovered that toxic corporate culture was one of the main predictors of employee turnover during the Great Resignation.[2] Toxic workplaces were a primary reason people were leaving their jobs. The researchers also identified the top five characteristics of toxic workplaces. They are disrespectful, noninclusive, unethical, cutthroat, and abusive.[3]

Scholars haven't come to a consensus on how to define "toxic workplace" or what the key indicators are. But many of us know from experience that it's really difficult to do good work in bad environments. Even when we're participating with God in his redemptive work to rebuild, renew, and restore what has been broken, work can still be awful. We're not immune to work hurt. Neither were Nehemiah and the people of Judah who had returned to build the wall. They did their work in a toxic environment, and their story offers us wisdom for how we can respond when our workplace culture is unhealthy.

> *Toxic workplaces are disrespectful, non-inclusive, unethical, cutthroat, and abusive.*
> MIT SLOAN MANAGEMENT REVIEW

SANBALLAT THE WORKPLACE BULLY

What we've seen in the story of Nehemiah isn't a one-to-one correspondence with the modern workplace. Nehemiah didn't hire the people of Judah to work on the wall. They weren't all part of a big construction company. While they had some structure to organize their work—Nehemiah at the helm—we need to examine the political system in which they were operating to understand the intricacies of their toxic work environment.

In Nehemiah's day, Judah was a province of Persia. So was neighboring Samaria. Both were once their own countries with their own cultures, but Babylon and then Persia conquered them, setting up local rulers to keep the peace, collect taxes, and oversee their territory. When Nehemiah left the court of Artaxerxes to return to build the wall, he asked for "letters to the governors of Trans-Euphrates" so that they would give him safe passage to Judah (Nehemiah 2:7). Artaxerxes sent the letters and gave Nehemiah an armed escort as well. Unfortunately, the letters weren't as persuasive as Nehemiah had hoped. Nehemiah 2:10 tells us, "When Sanballat the Hornet and Tobiah the Ammonite official heard about this, they were very much disturbed that someone had come to promote the welfare of the Israelites." Sanballat was the governor of Samaria, and Tobiah likely worked underneath him. Scholars think that Sanballat could have felt threatened by Nehemiah's return and the work to rebuild Jerusalem.[4] This is not to mention that a reestablished and self-sufficient Jerusalem could have a negative economic impact on neighboring Samaria.

Sanballat and Tobiah were so disturbed by what Nehemiah intended to do in Jerusalem that they actively attempted to thwart the work of rebuilding. After Nehemiah presented the people of Judah with his plans to rebuild the wall, Sanballat, Tobiah, and their friend Geshem the Arab tried to instill fear in the Israelites. Nehemiah recalled, "They mocked us and ridiculed us. 'What is this you are doing?' They asked. 'Are you rebelling against the king?'" (Nehemiah 2:19). But Nehemiah wasn't deterred. He responded to them saying, "The God of heaven will give us success. We his servants will start rebuilding, but as for you, you have no share in Jerusalem or any claim or historic right to it" (Nehemiah 2:10). Nehemiah wasn't going to waste his breath engaging a fight when he had important work to do.

Once the work on the wall got underway, Sanballat and Tobiah cranked up their attacks. Nehemiah 4 begins with Sanballat in a fiery rage. Sanballat called the Israelites feeble and questioned their ability to rebuild the wall from the ruins. Tobiah joined in the mockery by insulting their work—"even a fox climbing up on it would break down their wall of stones" (Nehemiah 4:3). Once again, Nehemiah chose not to engage them. He didn't fight back. Instead he prayed and kept the work moving forward. "So we rebuilt the wall till all of it reached half its height, for the people worked with all their heart" (Nehemiah 4:6).

Sanballat and friends did not like the fact that the wall was going up. The cruel and threatening words weren't working. This time

Judah's enemies resorted to violence: "When [they] heard that the repairs to Jerusalem's walls had gone ahead and that the gaps were being closed, they were very angry. They all plotted together to come and fight against Jerusalem and stir up trouble against it" (Nehemiah 4:7-8). Morale among the Israelites began to fall. The work was tough. The threats made it tougher. The people complained to Nehemiah, "The strength of the laborers is giving out, and there is so much rubble that we cannot build the wall" (Nehemiah 4:10). Sanballat's threats were also getting to them. They feared being attacked while they worked (Nehemiah 4:11). Yet the work had to continue.

So Nehemiah made arrangements for the people of Judah to defend themselves and their families. He appointed some people to stand guard "behind the lowest points of the wall at the exposed places" and armed them with swords, spears, and bows (Nehemiah 4:13). In the places where the wall was weak, Nehemiah sent reinforcements. In the places where the peoples' hearts were weak, Nehemiah gave encouragement. He told the people, "'Don't be afraid of them. Remember the Lord, who is great and awesome, and fight for your families, your sons and your daughters, your wives and your homes" (Nehemiah 4:14). Nehemiah was right. The people of God never had to lift a hand to their enemies because God fought for them. God defended them and kept them safe.

Even still, the Israelites continued their work in a defensive posture. Nehemiah described how they did their work in this toxic environment filled with threats of violence:

> From that day on, half of my men did the work, while the other half were equipped with spears, shields, bows and armor. The officers posted themselves behind all the people of Judah who were building the wall. Those who carried materials did their work with one hand and held a weapon in the other, and each of the builders wore his sword at his side as he worked. (Nehemiah 4:16-18)

Even though the people were very spread out around the perimeter of the city, they had a plan to come together at the sound of a trumpet and a reminder, "Our God will fight for us!" (Nehemiah 4:20). When Nehemiah and the Israelites were rebuilding the wall, they were working in a battle zone.

WHEN WORK FEELS LIKE A BATTLE ZONE

Toxic work environments can also feel like a battle zone. We've got to do our jobs while keeping up our defenses. Just ask Molly. In her job as a floral designer, she had a boss who would regularly yell at the staff, slam papers on her desk, or shove things off the counter. Molly felt anxious every day she went to work, keeping her guard up in case she was on the receiving end of her boss's wrath.

Toxic workplaces can be exhausting and cause both psychological and physical harm. In her article for *Harvard Business Review*, Manuela Priesemuth wrote that toxic workplaces can lead to "decreased satisfaction, productivity, and commitment to the job as well as the organization at large."[5] Researchers Vicki Webster, Paula Brough, and Kathleen Daly found that we can experience anxiety and depression, emotional harm, and physical health issues when we work for toxic bosses.[6]

When she took the job as children's ministries director, Sarah never anticipated that her church would turn out to be a toxic work environment, one that would eventually drive her to quit after five years on the job. She built a capable team and a thriving ministry in a large church. She was flourishing right up until she had a difficult encounter with another staff member. When she asked both of their supervisors to intervene and help them resolve their issues, she had to wait six weeks for them to set a meeting. She recalled how the meeting began, with the other staff member yelling at her while the supervisors and a human resources representative did nothing to intervene. Sarah left the meeting without any sort of resolution. She wanted someone to help mediate conflict and to say that the staff member's behavior was unacceptable. But no one did. Sarah realized that her supervisors weren't her advocates. Their inaction resulted in decreased trust and damaged the relationship that she had with them.

Sarah loved her job, her team, and the families they served. She had been successful in her role. She wondered, "Is this place actually toxic? Is it just me? Am I the only one who sees this?" It took Sarah about nine months to discern that the environment was, in fact, toxic. In the two-and-a-half years she had been in her full-time role, these were some of the messages she explicitly and implicitly received from her workplace:

- We can easily replace you.
- We don't care about you.
- We won't advocate for you.
- We'll take credit for your work.
- We won't take care of our people.

Brian, Molly, and Sarah aren't alone. For years my mom worked for a tyrant who yelled at his direct reports. Another elementary school teacher told me how, when she was hired by her district, the administration told her how lucky she was to have a job because of the long line of applicants trying to work there. A friend working in a faith-based nonprofit shared that her boss threatened to write her up for not loving her enough. Toxic. Toxic. Toxic.

DECIDING WHETHER TO STAY OR GO

What do we do when we're caught in a toxic work environment? In 1972, Princeton professor Albert O. Hirschman wrote a book called *Exit, Voice, and Loyalty: Responses to Decline in Organizations, Firms, and States*, which laid the groundwork for understanding four options we have when we're dissatisfied with our employer: exit, voice, loyalty, and neglect.[7] First, we can exit. This could be in the form of quitting or requesting a transfer. Second, we can stay and use our voice to advocate for change. Third, we can remain loyal, "suffer in silence," and hope things will improve.[8] Fourth, we can neglect or become lax in our work.

Not all options are equal. Our contexts and constraints may limit what we can do. If we worked hard to obtain our position, we might be reluctant to leave. Alternatively, we may have to choose voice or loyalty if we can't quickly move into a new position. But using our voice could get us fired. Neglect can put raises, promotions, references, and even our jobs in jeopardy. Each option comes with potential risks and rewards, and each option needs to be weighed carefully in a process of vocational discernment. Before we make a decision, we can take some time to check in with God, with friends and mentors, and with ourselves. We can also apply some of the wisdom we learn from Nehemiah.

PRAY AND ASK GOD TO INTERVENE

First, when we find ourselves in a toxic work environment or working for a toxic leader, we can pray. That's what Nehemiah did. Let's examine his prayer:

> Hear us, our God, for we are despised. Turn their insults back on their own heads. Give them over as plunder in a land of captivity. Do not cover up their guilt or blot out their sins from your sight, for they have thrown insults in the face of the builders. (Nehemiah 4:4-5)

First, he asked God to attend to his prayer. Then he said why. Next, he asked God to beat up his bullies.

This is an imprecatory prayer. Imprecatory prayers are a plea for vengeance, a "cry for justice."[9] The book of Psalms contains several imprecatory prayers, notably Psalm 137, which speaks of the Babylonian exile. That's the one that ends with, "Happy is the one who seizes your infants and dashes them against the rocks" (Psalm 137:9). Brutal! The Israelites living in captivity were despondent. So they prayed for God's righteous judgment on Babylon and her inhabitants, big and small. In his prayer, Nehemiah asked for God's judgment on Sanballat and his friends.

It may feel awkward, even violent, to pray for the demise of those who harm us. Tish Harrison Warren admits, "An imprecation is a curse. The imprecatory psalms are those that call down destruction, calamity, and God's judgment on enemies. Honestly, I don't usually know what to do with them. . . . I am often uncomfortable with the violence and self-assured righteousness found in these kinds of psalms."[10] Reflecting on the brutality of Russia's war on Ukraine, Warren goes on to say, "But [these prayers] were made for moments like these." What we experience in our workplaces may seem like a far cry from war, but toxic leaders and toxic workplaces crush people—perhaps not with the weight of a thousand bombs but definitely with the heaviness of shame, guilt, fear, and anxiety caused by the leaders' bullying, gaslighting, and harassment.

Theologian Brent A. Strawn reminds us, "It is far better to pray vengeful thoughts than take vengeful action."[11] When we're in a toxic situation at work, we can pray to God for help. We can ask God to change our situation. *Dear Lord, deliver me from this place, or at least deliver me from having to report to Cynthia for another minute.* We can ask God to set all of the wrongs to right and to judge those responsible for treating us poorly. *God on High, look down on us and see our misery. We're overworked and underpaid. Deal swiftly with those who profit off our oppression.* Yet even as we call on God to act, God calls us through Christ to love our enemies and pray *for* those who persecute us (Matthew 5:44). *You are a God who does miracles. Lord, you see how Brad has bullied me every day. Transform his heart with your mercy. Help him to experience joy in his work today.* When the Israelites were in captivity, God told them to pray for the flourishing of those around them. We can do that too.

PUT ON THE FULL ARMOR OF GOD

When Sanballat and his friends continued to threaten the people of God, Nehemiah armed them for battle. The application for us today is not a call to arms. The U.S. Bureau for Labor Statistics reports that in 2020, there were nearly four hundred deaths and forty thousand nonfatal injuries due to workplace violence.[12] We don't need any more of that type of work hurt. But Scripture teaches of an armor that God gives us to fight against every sort of enemy we encounter in this life.

The apostle Paul calls us to "Put on the full armor of God" (Ephesians 6:11). He continues by telling us that our enemies actually aren't people, rather they're spiritual forces that are opposed to God and his work in the world. Sanballat and his buddies, toxic people in toxic workplaces—they're not the real enemy. The battle we're in is ultimately spiritual; therefore, we need weapons of a different kind.

The armor of God is a word picture Paul gave us to help us envision what it looks like for the Christian to gear up for battle against the spiritual forces that oppose God. God has given us what we need to endure the fight. But we actually have to put it on. Preparation requires action and participation on our part. And that action and participation must align with the marks of God's kingdom. New Testament scholar Klyne Snodgrass summarizes:

> To do evil to people does not fit with the Christian faith. We may not suddenly forget tolerant love, patience, and peace when we encounter people doing wrong. We still are defined by and armed with truth, righteousness, readiness, faith, and the gospel, not ill-will, slander, anger, and violence. The way we carry on our battles is the most eloquent witness to our faith.[13]

When employed in toxic workplaces, we're equipped and called to respond in a uniquely Christian way.

We've got to go back to the truth of God's Word to remember who he is, who we are in his eyes, and how he's created work to be. We've got to pray, believing that the Spirit of God is going ahead of us and doing battle on our behalf with more strength and power than we could ever muster on our own. We've got to act rightly, do justly, and find avenues for showing mercy even when it's difficult.

And here's the good news: we don't have to do it alone. Paul's call wasn't to individual believers. This isn't a solo fight. Paul called all of us to put on the armor of God. We should all be actively engaged in this battle daily, regardless of how much toxicity we individually experience in our workplaces. We can take a stand for righteousness, goodness, truth, and beauty on a daily basis and pray for God's peace to cover the earth as waters cover the sea (see Habakkuk 2:14). We can love our enemies and pursue reconciliation armed with the power of the gospel, which is a unifying force (Ephesians 2:11-22).

> *We can take a stand for righteousness, goodness, truth, and beauty on a daily basis and pray for God's peace to cover the earth as waters cover the sea.*

A CAUTION ABOUT CALLING

In addition to prayer and the armor of God, a sense of calling can help us endure a difficult work environment. Elaine Howard Ecklund, Brenton Kalinowski, and Denise Daniels found this to be true in their research on work and calling. They shared,

> Teachers talked about dealing with the bureaucracy of state educational systems, and medical service workers discussed the daily grind of mopping floors and handling bodily waste. However, despite the challenges of their work, these people also acknowledged that they were able to get through the

Working in a Battle Zone 127

day-to-day aspects of their jobs because they felt spiritually called to their work.[14]

However, if we're not careful, what we believe about calling can cause more harm than good.

First, we can be tempted to think that sensing a calling exempts us from trouble and hardship in our work. That's not consistent with what we read in Scripture. We've seen it in the story of the Israelites trying to rebuild Jerusalem. God called them home to work on the temple and the wall, but bullies threatened them with words and acts of violence. Jesus promised his disciples, "In this world you will have trouble" (John 16:33). Following Jesus can and does put us in harm's way. So when we're tempted to leave a job because we think a sense of calling entitles us to an easy life, we need to remember that calling does not negate hardship. In fact, responding to God's invitation sometimes takes us straight into the heart of danger and difficulty.

Second, while a sense of calling to a particular job or role can help us endure a challenging situation, it can also lock us into inaction. In their research, Ecklund, Kalinowski, and Daniels also found that sensing a calling to a particular job or role can hinder our ability to take action when the work environment is unhealthy. They refer to this phenomenon as the "double-edged sword" of calling, a concept previously coined by calling researchers J. Stuart Bunderson and Jeffrey A. Thompson.[15] We can suffer or sacrifice unnecessarily in our work in the name of calling. We can assume that God wants us to grin and bear it when actually God's invitation may be for us to advocate for change or leave.

PRACTICE COURAGE

Sometimes we may not be able to leave our toxic workplaces. Other times, God may call us to stay in order to be agents of change within them. Regardless, we need courage to stand while we take on the full armor of God. Author and therapist K.J. Ramsey knows courage. She's had to demonstrate it in the face of numerous health challenges, and she and her husband weathered time in a toxic church.

In her book *The Lord is My Courage*, K.J. reflects on the story of David's battle with Goliath as she writes about courage. She describes courage as "the practice of wanting to protect what is good and true and beautiful more than we want to avoid being wounded. Courage is not the absence of anxiety but the practice of trusting that we will be held and loved no matter what happens."[16] Practicing courage is hard work. We're not the cowardly lion in *The Wizard of Oz*, who receives the gift of courage and automatically has the bravery of the king of beasts. We're humans, and we have to muster courage—sometimes by doing painful inner work and preparation—before we take our stand. Courage is also difficult because it requires us to "hold hurt and hope," Ramsey writes.[17] She says, "Courage is a continuous choice to be honest with the reality of harm while reaching for hope."[18] That's precisely the work of staying in toxic workplaces—knowing that we likely can and will be harmed but also believing that God is working beyond what we can see. That's also the work of leaving toxic workplaces behind—acknowledging the hurt they caused while at the same time trusting that we'll find God's provision on the other side.

Sarah demonstrated courage when faced with a toxic situation at her church. She pursued truth and reconciliation knowing that she would have to face the coworker who lashed out at her in the process. She demonstrated hope while she nursed her hurt. Even though the situation didn't come to a peaceful resolution, and Sarah eventually quit, she was able to heal from her hurt over time. Now she leads an adult discipleship ministry from her home, using the gifts, experience, and training God has given her.

Doug stayed in a toxic work situation for over four years. Six months into his job as an insurance agent, Doug's boss, Janet, began to criticize him regularly via Slack and in their one-on-one meetings.

A high performer and well-liked throughout the company for his integrity and kindness, Doug worked diligently to meet his quarterly sales goals, develop new customer relationships, and expand the business. So it didn't make sense to Doug when Janet made snide remarks about his sales tactics or wanted to dwell on the potential new customers he didn't land as opposed to celebrating his wins. Additionally, even though Doug received glowing reviews from his direct reports, Janet made him feel like he was a terrible manager. He knew he wasn't perfect, but he couldn't understand what he was doing wrong. No matter how well he performed, Janet would find something to nitpick. A friend suggested that perhaps Janet felt threatened by him, but Doug wasn't out to take her job. He just wanted to do well at his.

> *Courage is a continuous choice to be honest with the reality of harm while reaching for hope.*
>
> K.J. RAMSEY

When he considered his options, Doug felt stuck. His family relied on his income and the benefits he got through his employer. He couldn't just walk away without another job lined up. Plus, he knew that staying in the job for a few years would help his chances of getting a better job when it was time to leave. So he stayed and tried to continue doing his best work. Some days Janet was so awful to him that he cried out to God for mercy. He also prayed for Janet and asked God to give him the eyes to see her as a person. Maybe she was dealing with insecurity, a difficult family situation, or her own work hurt. Over time, Doug's mental health began to deteriorate. He wasn't sleeping well because his mind raced all night trying to come up with ways to respond to or avoid Janet's judgment. Doug realized that, barring a miracle, her behavior toward him wouldn't change. So he started looking for an exit.

REMEMBER WHO WINS

Toxic workplaces can make us physically, emotionally, and spiritually sick. They can make us question our sense of calling. Some of us have the ability to escape them. Others don't. A few are called to stay and fight for change. But toxic workplaces don't have to be the death of us. God is on our side, hearing our prayers for justice, suiting us with spiritual armor, and filling our hearts with courage. If we skip to the end of Nehemiah, we see that Sanballat the workplace bully didn't thwart God's plans as much as he tried. Brick by brick, armed with sword and spear, the Israelites rebuilt the wall around Jerusalem. Our modern workplaces may feel like a battle zone with threats on every side. Do not lose heart: the Lord is with us and for us in our good work.

WORK HURT CLINIC

Symptoms: Which of the following have you experienced at work?

- Bullying
- Harassment
- Discrimination
- Harsh criticism
- Unethical culture
- Unhealthy culture
- Angry outbursts or displays

Have you experienced them intermittently or chronically?

Pain:

- How would you describe the emotional, physical, and spiritual suffering you have experienced as a result?
- How would you rate your pain?

Care:

- Practice vocational discernment when deciding whether to stay or go.
- Pray and ask God to intervene.
- Ask God to change your situation.
- Ask God to set the wrongs to rights.
- Pray for the boss, colleague, client, vendor, or leader responsible for making your workplace toxic.

Working in a Battle Zone

- Put on the full armor of God.
- Prayerfully consider if you're suffering unnecessarily in a toxic work environment.
- Practice courage.
- Remember that God ultimately wins the battle.

8

Being Exploited and Oppressed

FOR MANY OF US, it's difficult to imagine life before Amazon.com, Inc. I remember when Amazon became famous as a low-price bookseller. Back then, Amazon.com earned just over $14 billion in net sales revenue. In 2022 the corporation reported a net sales revenue of over $500 billion and now sells everything from books and bananas to treadmills and tennis shoes.[1]

Unfortunately, Amazon.com has come under scrutiny for how it treats its employees. Some employees have complained about how heavily Amazon monitors their work activity and productivity. The *Washington Post* reported, "High-tech monitoring presses warehouse staff to meet onerous metrics and can lead to injuries, workers and regulators have said."[2] In March 2023, the National Employment Law Project reported, "Amazon warehouse workers are injured at almost double the rate of non-Amazon warehouse workers in Massachusetts."[3] That same year, the Occupational Safety and Health Administration, part of the U.S. Department of Labor, found Amazon.com guilty of unsafe working conditions at several warehouse locations.[4]

Big box retailers aren't the only companies guilty of creating harsh or oppressive workplaces for their employees. Small businesses do it too. Shortly after graduating from high school, Julia began working part-time at her gym, a franchise owned by a small company that ran several locations in the region. She did a variety of tasks including signing up new members and cleaning the equipment. She enjoyed her job and loved interacting with the people she met there. In a little over a year, she was promoted to assistant manager and then to general manager.

Naturally, Julia's responsibilities increased as she moved up the organizational hierarchy, but so did her stress. As a general manager, she was responsible for hiring and training new employees, enlisting personal trainers, advertising for the gym, recruiting new members, meeting sales quotas, and doing most of the cleaning. She recalls never receiving formal management training for her role. Yet, from what she told me, she was good at her job. Her rapid promotion to manager signaled to me that her employers thought so too.

Julia's biggest complaint was that the franchise owner had little to nothing in the way of human resources policies or personnel. No one seemed to care about fair compensation and safe working conditions. The company had trouble staffing their gym locations. As a result, Julia typically worked well over forty hours per week. Yet she made only about $30,000 a year. Even though she was a salaried employee, she did not receive benefits like health insurance and retirement contributions. She was even asked to run multiple gyms simultaneously for a few months and received no additional pay.

Julia's work also felt physically unsafe to her at times. She was asked to clean underneath the gym's treadmills, which would have required lifting them. According to the job description for a gym manager at a different nationwide gym franchise, the maximum weight a manager would be asked to lift at work is seventy-five pounds. A commercial treadmill weighs approximately four hundred pounds if not more. Julia was also asked to rent and operate a lift in order to clean the air vents. She didn't know if she could sign a rental agreement because she was only nineteen years old, and she was afraid she would not be able to operate the machine without breaking it or damaging the gym equipment or facility.

Eventually, Julia confided in her boss that she felt overwhelmed in her role. She said she was having a difficult time coming to work and maintaining a positive attitude throughout her day. Instead of offering support, her boss wrote her up for having a poor attitude and put her on a performance improvement plan. Julia was told by her boss that her next infraction would result in termination. Unwilling to work under the threat of being fired, Julia quit.

OPPRESSIVE AND EXPLOITATIVE WORK

The world of work is ripe for oppression and exploitation. It starts young—even among children. Older siblings demand that younger siblings get them a snack or ask mom to do this or that. It's easy to pass the work we don't want to do onto the least of these among us. Work hurt hits the vulnerable among us harshly. Unfortunately, millions of people around the world—adults and children—work in oppressive and exploitative conditions including low-wage work, precarious work, hazardous work, and forced labor. But that doesn't have to be their story.

> *Millions of people around the world—adults and children—work in oppressive and exploitative conditions including low-wage work, precarious work, hazardous work, and forced labor.*

LOW-WAGE WORK

As of January 2024, 12 percent of US workers made fifteen dollars per hour or less. During the Covid-19 pandemic, the essential nature of many of their jobs came into sharp relief because they did not

Being Exploited and Oppressed 135

have the option to stay at home when everyone else did.[5] Low-wage workers include retail sales associates, grocery store cashiers, custodians, nursing assistants, and dishwashers. Though vital to the economy, these individuals often feel trapped in their positions, unable to gain the education and skills needed to advance into higher wage jobs.[6] They may also work irregular and inflexible schedules and have limited access to health care and other benefits.

Pamela is a single mother. She works as a medical assistant at the local hospital. She's required to clock in at 8 a.m., but she has to take her three daughters to school first. Some days, she struggles to get everyone out of the house on time, and she begins her morning frazzled, knowing that her employer has no tolerance for her being fifteen minutes late. She wants to care for her children and give them all a better life, but she worries that one tough morning could make her lose her job. Meanwhile, some of the hospital's salaried employees can drop their kids off at school, take their time getting to work, and leave in the middle of the day to attend their first grader's class play without fear of consequences. In addition to fearing what will happen if she doesn't arrive on time, Pamela feels frustrated by the inequity in the hospital's attendance policy.

PRECARIOUS WORK

Precarious work can be a subtle form of workplace exploitation. The word *precarious* means insecure, unpredictable, undependable, and likely to fall or collapse. Precarious work then is nonpermanent, insecure, unpredictable, or undependable types of employment. The amount of precarious work is growing as employers reduce their permanent workforce and hire instead temporary, contingent, or on-call employees.[7] Jobs secured through a temp agency, contract work, on-call work, seasonal work, and self-employment are forms of precarious work.[8]

The International Labour Organization describes the perils of precarious work this way:

Workers are forced to bear the risk of any downturn in the employer's business (because workers can be disposed of immediately when they're no longer needed). Yet even when they are working, workers can't plan their lives or support their families: their hours and schedules are undependable, and their pay and benefits are rock bottom. Many of these jobs fail to pay normal employment benefits like health, life insurance, sick pay, or pensions.[9]

As I mentioned, precarious work can be a subtle form of exploitation. I know because I've experienced it.

One of my friends once called me "Queen of the Side Hustle" because of all of the gig work I did. I was in the throes of precarious work for over a decade. I worked part-time at a clothing store, at which my manager would never schedule me for more than twenty-nine hours per week even though I had the availability and the store needed help. I also took freelance jobs writing problems for math tests. After I finished my doctorate, I became an adjunct professor. The technical term is contingent faculty. I shuddered the first time someone used that term because I felt it in my bones. I love teaching, and I was thrilled for the opportunity. But the pay was atrocious. One school I taught for even had a "kill fee" in their teaching contract. If the school needed to cancel the class due to low enrollment, they would pay me a couple of hundred dollars for my preparation work. What was I supposed to do about the rest of the lost income?

I didn't feel the full weight of precarious labor until I became our family's primary earner. Between working as an adjunct professor and being self-employed through my consulting business, which relied on contract work, I had to make enough money to meet our monthly expenses. Not having a consistent paycheck was so stressful. But the worst was when I applied for a mortgage and was denied. Denied. The first bank we approached when moving to Georgia wouldn't loan me a cent. I sobbed. It didn't matter that I had excellent credit or that we had owned two homes previously. It didn't matter that our income level had not changed. I was deemed a risky borrower because my income was unstable and unpredictable.

University of Illinois Chicago professor Vanessa Oddo found that precarious employment increased by 9 percent in the United States between 1988 and 2016.[10] Health researchers like Oddo have learned that precarious employment can adversely affect workers' well-being. It "can result in insufficient income, which compromises access to food and other necessities; greater exposure to adverse physical working conditions, such as toxic exposure, and limited control over both personal and professional lives, leading to stress."[11] The International Labour Organization reports that women can be particularly affected by precarious work because employers seek to take advantage of their desires to balance work and family life. Precarious work can be exploitative and can hurt workers. The damage it does is often financial but can be emotional and physical as well.

HARSH WORKING CONDITIONS

Having to work in harsh or unsafe working conditions is another type of exploitation and oppression. The fast-fashion industry is well known for this. *Fast fashion* is "the rapid production of clothing, generally in a way that sacrifices quality for quantity."[12] Several of today's popular clothing brands for both children and adults fall under the "fast fashion" label. I have some of those brands in my closet, and I've purchased them for my kids. School uniform shirts for five dollars. Jeans for eight dollars. Cheap clothes can be hard to resist.

Fast fashion has gotten a bad rap for how it treats its workers. University of Michigan professor Ravi Anupindi explains why manufacturing overseas is so attractive to global retailers: "On a $30 shirt, for example, a typical retailer markup is close to 60%. The factory makes a profit of $1.15, and the worker makes barely 18 cents. Were a similar shirt produced in the United States, labor costs would be closer to $10."[13] In this hypothetical model, it is fifty-six times more expensive for a company to produce a shirt in the United States than it is overseas. Cheap labor is alluring to many businesses. It's no surprise then that less than 2 percent of the 75 million factory workers in the fashion industry earn a living wage.[14]

Additionally, many fast-fashion workers labor in unsafe and unhealthy conditions. In 2013, Rana Plaza, a building in Bangladesh housing four garment factories and hundreds of other shops collapsed, killing over 1,100 people and injuring thousands more. Writing about the disaster for *Time*, Charlie Campbell captured the high cost of cheap fashion saying, "in order for consumers in developed economies to enjoy tasteful clothes at affordable prices, low-paid workers in countries like Bangladesh must toil in dangerous, sometimes lethal, conditions."[15]

In the United States, we may see the words "made in the U.S.A." on a label and assume that our clothing has been made by people who work in safe conditions and earn a living wage. However, the U.S. Department of Labor's Wage and Hour Division discovered in 2023 that 80 percent of garment industry contractors in Southern California "were violating minimum wage and overtime laws." One company was paying their employees less than two dollars per hour.[16] Fast fashion and its associated global brands aren't the only industry and companies that expose their workers to exploitative and oppressive conditions. Each year, the National Council for Occupational Safety and Health reports on the "Dirty Dozen"—twelve companies that put their workers and communities at risk. Their 2023 list includes Amazon, FedEx, Tesla, and a major player in the US rail industry.[17]

FORCED LABOR

Forced labor is the most exploitative and oppressive type of work. Here's an official definition: Forced labor is any "work that is undertaken both under the threat of any penalty and is involuntary. . . .

There must be both a lack of free and informed consent and coercion for work to be statistically regarded as forced labour."[18] It's considered a form of modern slavery that affects more women than men. Approximately three million of those in forced labor are children. Also, research indicates that forced labor is experienced by people of all social classes.[19] Over half of forced labor takes place in Asia and the Pacific and about 13 percent takes place in the Americas. In the private sector, the majority of forced labor happens in the service industry (excluding domestic work), manufacturing, construction, and agriculture. Migrant workers make up about 15 percent of the forced labor population globally.

Within the United States, immigrants and migrant workers are most susceptible to forced labor. The U.S. Department of Homeland Security reports that seven out of ten of those who have experienced forced labor in the United States entered the country legally.[20] Employers take advantage of their need for work, poor English language skills, and lack of knowledge of labor laws to coerce them into exploitative circumstances. Migrant farmworkers seeking to earn money so they may send it home to their families are particularly at risk. In November 2021, *The Atlanta Journal-Constitution* reported that government officials rescued twenty-six migrant workers from a farm in South Georgia. Those who attended to the victims learned that these workers had received little food and medical care while working on the farm.[21] Unfortunately, these migrants were part of larger modern-day slavery operation in rural Georgia. Officials brought a federal indictment against many of the conspirators for human trafficking and criminal mistreatment, among other charges.[22]

Workplace oppression and exploitation come in many forms. Researchers estimate that one in five workers in forced labor situations are in debt bondage—"when people are coerced to work against their will to repay a debt with an employer or recruiter, *or* when debt is manipulated to compel people to perform work tasks or accept work conditions that they would otherwise refuse."[23] In the book of Nehemiah, we see a particular type of forced labor similar to debt bondage. Sadly, oppressive and exploitative work took place among the people of God as they were trying to build a new life and a new city for themselves.

DISCOVERING EXPLOITATION IN JERUSALEM

Global crises from worldwide recession to extreme weather provide the perfect opportunities for people to prey on the poor and vulnerable. The poor and vulnerable often work grueling hours to cover their heads and put a bit of food on the table. The tiniest upset in the global economy, the way they earn their living, or how they access their food threatens their survival. That's what the poor and vulnerable in Jerusalem experienced. In addition to being bullied by Sanballat and his buddies while rebuilding the wall, the poor and the vulnerable Israelites were exploited by the wealthy and powerful among them.

We don't learn until Nehemiah 5 that God's people were rebuilding the wall during a time of famine. While they were stacking brick on brick and repairing the city's gates, the people still had to feed their families. That meant that some of the people had to tend fields, harvest crops, and store excess grain. But there was no grain (Nehemiah 5:2). Some of the Israelites had to mortgage their property to afford food. Others had to take out loans to pay their taxes to the Persian government. And still some had to force their sons and daughters into

> *In addition to being bullied by Sanballat and his buddies while rebuilding the wall, the poor and the vulnerable Israelites were exploited by the wealthy and powerful among them.*

slavery to afford their debts. Who were the lenders, the slave owners, the land barons? Their fellow Jews, Nehemiah 5:5 tells us. If we skip ahead a few verses, we learn that it was specifically the Israelite nobles and officials. The wealthy and powerful were exploiting the poor and vulnerable among them in their time of need.

This made Nehemiah angry. He wanted to rebuke the nobles and officials, so he "called together a large meeting to deal with them" (Nehemiah 5:7). He couldn't believe what they were doing. When he called them out, the nobles and officials were speechless: "They kept quiet, because they could find nothing to say" (Nehemiah 5:8). Nehemiah told them, "'What you are doing is not right. Shouldn't you walk in the fear of our God to avoid the reproach of our Gentile enemies? I and my brothers and my men are also lending the people money and grain. But let us stop charging interest'" (Nehemiah 5:9-10).

The Bible says the nobles were charging "only one percent of the money, grain, new wine and olive oil" (Nehemiah 5:11). Modern-day interest rates make the interest rate mentioned in Nehemiah 5 sound absurdly low. A one percent interest rate may seem like a steal, but God's law forbade the Israelites to lend to one another with interest. After they had been delivered from Egypt, God commanded his people: "Do not charge a fellow Israelite interest, whether on money or food or anything else that may earn interest" (Deuteronomy 23:19). God had also given his people explicit instructions concerning the poor among them:

> If any of your fellow Israelites become poor and are unable to support themselves among you, help them as you would a foreigner and stranger, so they can continue to live among you. Do not take interest or any profit from them, but fear your God, so that they may continue to live among you. You must not lend them money at interest or sell them food at a profit. I am the LORD your God, who bought you out of Egypt to give you the land of Canaan and to be your God. (Leviticus 25:35-37)

The nobles and officials were breaking God's law and exploiting their brothers and sisters in the family of God during a time of need. Nehemiah would not allow it any longer. He didn't merely want the nobles and officials to stop charging interest, he wanted them to give back what they took. The nobles and officials agreed. But Nehemiah made them promise they wouldn't go back to their exploitative practices.

LEADING BY EXAMPLE

Nehemiah did not want to be numbered among the nobles who exploited their fellow Israelites. Instead, he opted for a different type of leadership. During the twelve years he served as governor of Judah, Nehemiah refused some of the benefits that came with the position. Notably, he and his brothers didn't eat their allotment of food (Nehemiah 5:14). He described how his practice differed from that of his predecessors. Those governors "placed a heavy burden on the people and took forty shekels of silver from them in addition to food and wine. Their assistants also lorded it over the people" (Nehemiah 5:15). Nehemiah continued by giving his motivation for not following in their footsteps: "But out of reverence for God I did not act like that" (Nehemiah 5:15).

Nehemiah obeyed God and concentrated on his work of rebuilding the wall. He didn't focus on getting rich and enjoying the trappings of nobility. Nehemiah also showed tremendous generosity. He regularly prepared feasts that he shared with dozens of fellow Israelites, officials, and visitors from surrounding nations. Even in hosting these lavish meals, Nehemiah recalled, "I never demanded the food allotted to the governor because the demands were heavy on these people" (Nehemiah 2:18). In a time of scarcity, he led with empathy and compassion.

MODERN-DAY MERCY GIVERS

It can be difficult if not impossible for oppressed and exploited workers to find better working conditions on their own. Even those in precarious work may not be able to shoulder the financial risk of leaving their current employment to find a new job. Think about the single parent who works through a temp agency while her children attend school. Not only would she have to miss work to interview for other jobs, a new job could require her to need more childcare or drive further to work. Or think about the young adult working in a dangerous warehouse job to get tuition benefits so he can attend college. Walking away from that job could mean walking away from his education as well. Those in exploitative situations like forced labor often need to be rescued—as was the case with the migrant farm workers in Georgia and is the case with millions around the globe bound in modern-day slavery. That's why folks in these situations often need modern-day mercy givers to help them change their situation.

Max De Pree was a modern-day mercy giver. His legacy influences leaders to this day. Max De Pree was the longtime CEO of Herman Miller Inc., a Michigan-based company that became famous for its midcentury modern office furniture. While Max was CEO of Herman Miller, the company became one of the most profitable among the Fortune 500. Yet Max didn't focus on amassing immense wealth for himself. Instead, he capped his salary at twenty times the wage of an hourly worker. By comparison, the Economic Policy Institute reports that in 2022, CEOs were paid approximately 344 times the pay of a typical worker.[24]

Max's Christian faith inspired not only his salary decision but also how he treated his employees. He believed in "a concept of persons" rooted in the fact that people are made in God's image. Leading a company meant believing that everyone in the organization had gifts to offer. Max celebrated "the intrinsic value of their diversity" and wanted to help everyone fulfill their potential.[25] Max enacted his beliefs through implementing the Scanlon Plan within Herman Miller. He created a way for employees to participate in profit sharing. He wrote,

Employee stock ownership is essential to a declaration of identity. Motivation is not a significant problem: Herman Miller employees bring that with them by the bushel. But people need to be liberated, to be involved, to be accountable, and to reach for their potential. . . . Stock ownership is a marvelous vehicle for involving an entire family in the career of those of us who work for corporations.[26]

To be sure, employee stock ownership is not without its risks, but it's a way to care for employees by helping them build wealth and participate in their work as stakeholders. As Nehemiah did, Max set an example for organizational leaders and managers: this is what it can look like to care for your employees well *and* promote their flourishing. If we have the capacity to support someone's well-being at work, we have a responsibility to do so. It's a practical outworking of "love your neighbor as you love yourself" (Matthew 22:39).

> *If we have the capacity to support someone's well-being at work, we have a responsibility to do so.*

EXTENDING COMPASSION TO EXPLOITED WORKERS

We don't have to be in a position of leadership or management to be modern-day mercy givers. We can love those who are entrapped in exploitative and oppressive labor through compassion, awareness, and advocacy. First, many of us have experienced the disappointment, disillusionment, and devastation work can cause. Our work wounds can give us eyes to see other forms of work hurt like exploitation and oppression. God can use the pain we've experienced at work to help us have compassion for those who may be stuck in exploitative circumstances.

Second, we can also become more aware—bringing our attention to what we're buying. First, we can examine our favorite brands' employment practices and make different choices about where and how we shop. Sometimes this can feel ethically complex for me because I tell myself that buying the cheap shirt helps someone feed their family or send their kids to school. But here's the deal: that person deserves a safer and better paying job. If I can play a small role by no longer contributing to the injustice they experience, that seems like a step in the right direction.

Advocacy is another way we can love our neighbor and fight against exploitative and oppressive labor practices. Advocacy can shape policy. The California Transparency in Supply Chains Act became law in 2010 because Californians expressed concern about how the products they purchased were made.[27] This law requires companies to inform the public of their efforts to "eradicate human trafficking and slavery within their supply chains."[28] Laws like this want companies and their consumers to be conscious of forced labor. At the time of this writing, the New York legislature is considering the Fashion Act, which also arose in response to consumer demand that global brands be more transparent about their supply chains.[29]

We can also be advocates in our workplaces. We can observe and listen to employee feedback and exit interviews to discern if any of our company's practices are potentially exploitative or oppressive. We can become familiar with the policy manuals in our organizations and courageously speak up if we discern an unjust rule or practice. And we can examine the pay and benefit structures for all positions—especially precarious workers—to ensure that everyone is compensated fairly and that their work is structured in a way that supports their well-being.

As a result of feeling exploited in her workplace, which she attributed to their lack of human resources policies and personnel, Julia decided to study human resources in college. She didn't want other employees to experience what she did. Instead she wanted to be their support and advocate. She wanted to be a modern-day mercy giver.

God wants his people to pursue justice for people who are exploited and oppressed. In Isaiah 58, God scolded his people because they did religious things like fast and pray while, at the same time, exploiting the poor and vulnerable among them. He reminded them that true worship requires works of mercy and justice:

> Is not this the kind of fasting I have chosen:
> to loose the chains of injustice
> and untie the cords of the yoke,
> to set the oppressed free
> and break every yoke?
> Is it not to share your food with the hungry
> and to provide the poor wanderer with shelter—
> when you see the naked, to clothe them,
> and not to turn away from your own flesh and blood?
> (Isaiah 58:6-7)

God told his people that their practices and their flourishing were intertwined. If they fought oppression and devoted themselves to serving the most vulnerable, then the Lord would guide them. Then they would "rebuild the ancient ruins" (Isaiah 58:9-12). Then they would "find [their] joy in the Lord" (Isaiah 58:14). They could not flourish individually unless they cared about the flourishing of everyone. We can change the story of exploited and oppressed workers. We can love them well—with our compassion, our awareness, and our advocacy—and do our part to help them experience work that's closer to what God designed it to be.

PRAYING FOR A SIGN

When we think of oppressive, exploitative, and unsafe working conditions, our minds probably conjure up images of crowded factories and stifling warehouses, not beautifully decorated, air-conditioned C-suite offices. Yet that's where Suzanne almost died, being overworked by a toxic boss who showed no regard for Suzanne's life or that of her unborn child. Suzanne got pregnant at the end of 2020. It was a high-risk pregnancy from the start, but the requirement to return to work in the office while Covid-19 rates were still high in her area added to Suzanne's stress. Along with that, her relationship with her boss was deteriorating rapidly.

When she was six months pregnant, Suzanne was desperate to leave, but she felt stuck. If she left without another job lined up, she wouldn't have health benefits that she desperately needed during her pregnancy and for the baby's birth. Plus she absolutely loved the company and didn't want to leave. A friend encouraged her to apply for another job, but she felt conflicted about leaving. *Should I stay at an organization I love with a boss I hate or go work for someone I love who won't kill me*? She ended up applying for the job when she was seven months pregnant, and she got it, but she wouldn't be eligible for benefits in the new role until she had been there for ninety days. That meant she couldn't accept the new job. With a baby coming soon, she needed health insurance. She would have to wait.

With four days left to work before she went on maternity leave, Suzanne contracted Covid-19. She was thirty-six weeks pregnant. She was so sick that she could barely get out of bed. Yet her boss demanded that she work. She called Suzanne frequently to make sure that she was helping the new employee learn the job. Contracting Covid-19 while pregnant was dangerous, especially for someone with a high-risk pregnancy. Every other day, Suzanne had to go to the hospital for tests. She kept getting sicker. She desperately needed to rest. Suzanne told me, "My boss was killing me."

Before her maternity leave was over, Suzanne learned that her boss had made an error when filling out the maternity leave paperwork. Suzanne would have to return to work one month before she had planned. What would she do about childcare? How could she return to work for such an awful boss? Suzanne felt so uncertain, so physically and emotionally exhausted. She had practically given up and lost hope. She wanted her job to be over. She prayed that God would give her a sign to stay or go.

She got one, a sign. Even though she had never accepted the offer at that other company, Suzanne's name was in the company's employee database. One day she came home to find a package from them—a holiday gift. That simple expression of care was the sign she needed. She quit her job, took the new one, and never looked back.

HOLD FAST TO GOD

Millions of people around the world long for deliverance from harsh, exploitative, and oppressive work conditions. If you find yourself among them, you are not alone. God is with you. When you cannot delight in the work of your hands, try to delight yourself in the Lord. Hold fast to him, the God who sees the exploited and oppressed. Hold fast to Jesus, who came to set the prisoners free. And pray for deliverance, trusting that God hears your cries.

WORK HURT CLINIC

Symptoms: In your work, have you ever been . . .
- exploited?
- oppressed?
- paid very low wages?
- forced to work in harsh or unsafe conditions?
- in a job that felt unstable or insecure?

Care:
- Commit to everyday faithfulness.
- Hold fast to God.

Realizing It's Me

I THINK THIS SITUATION HAPPENED when my husband and I were dating. We were hanging out when I caught of whiff of something putrid. It was body odor; I was sure of it. And I was also sure that it was not coming from me. I smell like sunshine and daffodils.

I asked, "What's that smell?" I'm sure in my tone I implied that it was him and not me. But it wasn't him. I subtly turned my nose toward my armpits and grimaced. Then I said with a loud, unfortunate sigh, "It's me!" (Insert the crying emoji.) I was so embarrassed. But that experience is a good reminder for me in moments when I'm tempted to lay blame on others. Maybe I'm the problem.

When it comes to work hurt, it's very easy and natural to point the finger at other people, systems, and organizations. It's the toxic bosses, competitive office cultures, and unexpected layoffs that are the problem. Yet sometimes, after the dust has settled from all the destruction, we realize the role we played in it.

REALIZING OUR ROLE IN WORK HURT

When Patrick quit his job as an adjunct professor, it was because of receiving low pay, feeling disrespected, and having no opportunities for advancement. At the time, those seemed like perfectly good reasons to leave. After the fact, he realized he could have done more to attempt to change his outcome. Even though he taught at the school for a few years, he never once initiated a conversation about his career goals or his hopes to progress in the profession and the organization. He never attempted to renegotiate his compensation. In the long run, he concluded his decision to leave was the right one, but he thinks he could have left better and with less hurt if he had clearly communicated his expectations and needs to his employer.

I've also known people who have inadvertently sabotaged their jobs out of a desire to look good to their bosses. Jane got fired from a nannying position because she was too afraid to ask for more clarity about what her employer expected of her. She said, "I was afraid asking questions would make me look incompetent, but I ended up doing that anyway." I've seen other people (myself included) burn out and contemplate quitting because they did way more work than asked or expected—again because they wanted to impress others.

To be fair, the emerging research on burnout emphasizes the workplace stressors that contribute to it. But we're sometimes our own worst enemy. In both my personal and professional life, I've had to monitor my compulsion to overwork—doing more than a boss, role, or task demands. When my boys were young, I thought that being a good mom meant serving them healthy, homemade snacks. I bought tiny little cookie cutters to make animal crackers from scratch. I love baking, but for me, that was overworking. Plus the packaged cookies taste better.

Professionally, overworking can look like taking on a project when I'm already maxed out because either I think I can do it faster and better than someone else or I want to be helpful. In an article for *Harvard Business Review*, Tony Schwartz and Eric Severson suggest a couple of reasons we can be prone to overwork:

We often experience a greater sense of our own value when we're working than we do when we're not. Working is not just a way to stay busy, but also to prove our worthiness—to others and to ourselves. Immersion in work helps hold off feelings of inadequacy, anxiety, loneliness, sadness, and emptiness that can arise when we have time off. We dread being bored.[1]

Our poor work habits, attitudes, and communication skills can contribute to the resentment, frustration, anger, and despair we feel in our work. But sometimes we can't see that "it's me" until it's too late. Other times, we know we're to blame right away—like when we make a mistake.

MISTAKES WITH BIG CONSEQUENCES

Hours before I interviewed Tom for this book, I discovered I had made a pretty big mistake at work. In my final check of our Giving Tuesday email, I overlooked that we didn't include a link or button that said, "donate here." I apologized to my boss and she was very gracious and gave me the chance to make it right. Fortunately our donors were very understanding. Tom wasn't so lucky when he made a mistake on the job in the early 1990s.

A few years out of college, Tom got a job with a large real estate brokerage firm. His role was to appraise properties to estimate what they were worth for tax purposes. After a few years on the job, a company filed a lawsuit against his brokerage alleging that Tom had overvalued a property. The truth of the matter was that Tom had overvalued it by accident because he wasn't careful in how he assessed a certain aspect of the property. His error added extra square footage to the building, throwing off its value. The other company accused him of fraud.

Tom's firm immediately put him on probation and kept a watchful eye over his work. During the litigation, he felt completely abandoned by his company. They showed no empathy to their young employee who had made an honest mistake and admitted it. Tom's boss's boss was angry, antagonistic, and wanted Tom gone. A few weeks later, he got his wish. Tom was fired and had to come home to his wife and infant daughter with no job.

Tom made a mistake. He admitted it. He never tried to cover it up or make excuses. Unfortunately, he had to face severe consequences. Whenever someone digs up that story to discredit him or question his work, he doesn't try to make himself look good or wallow in shame. Instead he tells the truth.

TRUTH TELLING

Truth telling isn't easy. It's difficult to take responsibility for our mistakes and missteps. We want to preserve our pride and peoples' perceptions of us. In the Bible, we see God's people engaging in several truth-telling practices. Three common ones are lament, confession, and praise. In lament, we're honest and open about our difficult circumstances and our pain. In confession, we tell the truth about personal, corporate, and systemic sinfulness—deeds done and left undone. In praise, we proclaim the truth about God to him.

> *In the Bible, we see God's people engaging in several truth-telling practices. Three common ones are lament, confession, and praise.*

When the walls around Jerusalem fell down, God's people used lament to tell the truth about their heartbreak and hold onto the hope that God still cared for them. When we encounter the Israelites in Nehemiah 7, the wall has been rebuilt and the doors put in place. The people are getting settled in the land. Nehemiah 8:1 tells us that they then asked Ezra the priest to read them the Law of Moses. Old Testament scholars believe that what was happening in this part of the story was a covenant renewal ceremony: the people were recommitting themselves to God.

Beginning on the first day of the seventh month (the date is important), Ezra began reading from the Book of the Law. The Levites explained the Scriptures to help the people understand. When they comprehended what was being taught in the Scriptures, the people wept. One scholar suggests that they wept because, upon hearing and understanding God's commands, they grieved over how lax they had been in their obedience.[2] Nehemiah, Ezra, and the Levites told the people not to weep but rather to celebrate and feast. Nehemiah said, "Do not grieve, for the joy of the LORD is your strength" (Nehemiah 8:10). The religious leaders didn't want the Israelites to dwell on their sin. They wanted them to delight in the grace of God.

The next morning, the people resumed listening to the Scriptures being read and explained. They got to the part where God prescribed the celebration of the Feast of Tabernacles. In our Bibles, we find these instructions in Leviticus 23:33-44. God commanded that the Israelites celebrate the feast beginning on the fifteenth day of the seventh month. The first and the eighth days were to be days of sabbath rest, and the people were to live in temporary shelters for seven days as a way to remember that the Israelites lived in temporary shelters when God brought them out of Egypt.

When they heard about the Feast of Tabernacles, the Israelites wanted to be obedient to the law. Since they were in the seventh month, they decided to celebrate the feast immediately. So they built temporary shelters for themselves and they held the festival for seven days (Nehemiah 8:16-18). The Scriptures record, "From the days of Joshua son of Nun until that day, the Israelites had not celebrated it like this. And their joy was very great" (Nehemiah 8:17).

These people had been through so much—the destruction of Jerusalem, exile in Babylon, threat of war while they rebuilt the wall, and famine throughout the land. Like the apostle Paul, they had been "hard pressed on every side" (2 Corinthians 4:8). Their circumstances had nearly zapped every ounce of their courage and strength. Then they heard the Word of the Law and knew the depth of their sin. Their hearts ached with remorse.

Then their grief turned to joy. How? By rehearsing with others the grace and goodness of God. In celebrating the Feast of Tabernacles, the Israelites remembered all the ways God had cared for his people since delivering them from Egypt. In the way that they lived for those seven days, they proclaimed the truth about God.

On the eighth day of the feast, they held an assembly. Nehemiah 9:1 tells us, "The Israelites gathered together, fasting and wearing sackcloth and putting dust on their heads." They also separated themselves from foreigners (Nehemiah 9:2). Through their behavior and dress, the Israelites demonstrated the attitudes of their hearts. They wanted to devote themselves to God, mourn their sins, and demonstrate that they were set apart for him alone. Nehemiah tells us that they confessed their sins and the sins of their ancestors (Nehemiah 9:2). In fact, they spent a quarter of the day in confession.

Nehemiah 9:5-37 records what the people prayed that day. Beginning with the creation of the heavens and the earth, the people proclaimed the mighty acts of God—how he chose Abram and made a covenant with him; how he delivered his people out of Egypt and guided them in the wilderness; and how he gave the law through Moses. They also confessed the sins of their ancestors calling them arrogant, stiff-necked, and disobedient (Nehemiah 9:16). And they remembered God's grace, proclaiming the covenant name God revealed to Moses: "a forgiving God, gracious and compassionate, slow to anger and abounding in love" (Nehemiah 9:17; see Exodus 34:6-7). The prayer describes the Israelite's history—the good and the bad: the ways God provided for them and the ways they rebelled against him. They also recalled what led to the destruction of Jerusalem and their exile:

> Stubbornly they turned their backs on you, became stiff-necked and refused to listen. For many years you were patient with them. By your Spirit you warned them through your

prophets. Yet they paid no attention, so you gave them into the hands of the neighboring peoples. But in your great mercy you did not put an end to them or abandon them, for you are a gracious and merciful God. (Nehemiah 9:29-31)

Their ancestors were to blame for the destruction of Jerusalem and the exile. They didn't just play *a* role in their hurt. They were entirely responsible for it.

The Israelites gathered praying in Jerusalem also acknowledged their shortcomings: "In all that has happened to us, you have remained righteous; you have acted faithfully, while we have acted wickedly" (Nehemiah 9:33). Truth. But not the whole truth. They had more to say to God. They were upset that they weren't free; Israel was still ruled by a foreign king.

Telling the truth is difficult. It's not easy to admit our faults, mistakes, or shortcomings and admit, at the same time, that we need help. Both require vulnerability and humility. Brené Brown writes, "Vulnerability sounds like truth and feels like courage."[3] That's right regardless of whether we're telling the truth to God or our boss— or even admitting it to ourselves.

> *Vulnerability sounds like truth and feels like courage.*
> — BRENÉ BROWN

OWNING OUR FAULTS

I don't know about you, but it's much easier for me to proclaim truths about God's character and saving acts than it is to be honest about my sins and shortcomings. Saying, "It's me!" and owning my part are not fun because I don't like to acknowledge or dwell on my faults. Who does? We all have blind spots, and it's hard to tell the truth about something you can't even recognize in your life. So how can we discover the role we might have played (or are currently playing) in our work hurt? I think we can begin by asking ourselves (or better yet having a friend or loved one ask us) some tough questions. The questions that follow come from my experience as both an employee and a manager. Not every question may apply to every work situation, but they can help us get to the truth.

The first set gets at issues that are a little more black and white.

- Did I make an error or mistake?
- Did I violate a protocol or policy?
- Did I speak or act in a way that was inconsistent with my organization's values or my profession's ethical standards?

This next series of questions revolves around communication.

- To what extent have I communicated to my supervisor about my needs, goals, and expectations?
- To what extent have I communicated to my supervisor about when and why I've felt frustrated, underappreciated, or overworked?
- To what extent have I asked questions and sought support to ensure I have the information and tools needed to do my job effectively?
- Have I communicated with kindness, honesty, humility, and self-control?

This set of questions is about work habits.

- How often do I do more work than is expected or required for a project? Why? What's my motivation?
- How often do I struggle to prioritize tasks and manage my workload? What supports might help me succeed?
- How much time do I spend working, resting, and playing in the course of a week?

This final set of questions is about attitude and fit.

- On average, how motivated am I to do my work well?
- On average, how excited am I about the work that I'm doing?
- To what extent are my skills and training a match for this job?

- To what extent do my values align with my organization's values?

FINDING OUR FIT

The last two questions use the words *match* and *align*. These are questions of fit. Up to this point, we haven't really discussed the concept of fit and how it relates to work. Let's start by thinking about shoes. I have narrow feet, which can make shoe-shopping painful, literally. My shoes need to be slim in the heel and roomy in the toe box. If the width isn't correct, I'll end up with blisters or the shoes will slip off while I'm walking. Fit matters in our shoes and in our work. The wrong fit can cause a job to rub us the wrong way. As we consider fit for certain roles, here are two dimensions of fit to consider.

Person-environment (P-E) fit is a psychological framework that seeks to explain how we interact with our environments, including the people in them. Vocational and industrial (or organizational) psychologists use P-E fit as a lens for understanding the types of organizations and jobs that lend themselves to higher job satisfaction, organizational commitment, motivation, performance, and other work outcomes for different individuals. The idea is that we'll naturally align in some places and roles better than others. Two types of P-E fit get the most attention. Generally speaking, person-organization (P-O) fit is the degree of alignment between us and our organization's values. For example, someone who had a strong sense of justice might work well in a nonprofit focused on advocacy or in the justice system. We have to be aware, though, that sometimes organizations can fail to practice their stated values. It happens in businesses, nonprofit organizations, churches, and educational institutions. Unfortunately, it can be difficult to discern the discrepancy between values and actions without speaking to other employees or working within the organization for a while.

Person-job (P-J) fit is the alignment between a person and the skills and abilities required for their job. My high school was selected to pilot test a new career assessment, and my results showed that I should be a hair stylist or do manual labor on an assembly line. Both are very fine and necessary jobs, but not for me. I may have cut my family's hair throughout the Covid-19 pandemic, but you do not want me getting near your head with clippers or a pair of scissors. My P-J fit would be rock-bottom in that case.

It may be worth evaluating our fit within our organization and our job. If the fit is off, it could contribute to poor job performance and low motivation, or stress and burnout. Bryan Dik and Ryan Duffy caution that we shouldn't make decisions about our work based on fit alone: "Fit is important, but it must absolutely be augmented by a broad appraisal of your personal context, your deepest values, the needs you see in the world that speak to your heart, the concerns you find most meaningful, and your personal life mission."[4] We may not always have the opportunity to work in jobs or organizations where we have high levels of fit. However, awareness of the environments in which we might thrive can help us discern if we need to engage in a little job crafting or have an "it's not you; it's me (but it's also a little bit you)" breakup conversation with our work. This sort of self-awareness is a form of truth telling.

> Fit . . . must absolutely be augmented by a broad appraisal of your personal context, your deepest values, the needs you see in the world that speak to your heart, the concerns you find most meaningful, and your personal life mission.
>
> **BRYAN DIK AND RYAN DUFFY**

Isabella is Jorge's wife. She immigrated to the United States with her parents when she was ten years old. In their home country of Venezuela, her mom was a doctor and her dad was an engineer. When they moved to the United States, her dad got a job at a large university. Her mom started a cleaning business. Isabella grew up helping her mom clean houses and offices on the weekends, but she saw her mom's exhaustion and realized she didn't want her life to look like that.

As a young adult, Isabella tried a handful of different careers, eventually falling in love with logistics. When her dad retired from the university, he decided to start a shipping business and invited Isabella to work with him. For years, Isabella tried to develop her own career while assisting both of her parents with theirs.

At thirty-four years old, Isabella realized that at times she felt frustrated and overwhelmed in her work. She loved helping her parents, but she didn't enjoy what she was doing. She felt obligated to join the family businesses out of loyalty to her parents who worked so hard to give their family a good life. But the work she was doing wasn't a good fit for her. So she started exploring new options—one of which was volunteering for an international organization. She came alive when she told me about it because in her role, she could use her college major along with all of the skills and experience she had gained in her previous work. Isabella had a learning mentality, and she used that plus her past and present work experiences to help her find her fit.

COMMITTING TO WORK DIFFERENTLY

After the Israelites had confessed their sins and acknowledged their wrongdoing, they committed to live differently. Nehemiah 10 describes an oath they made to God. They promised to follow the law and obey God's commands, to refrain from marrying people from other nations, to observe the Sabbath, to set aside money for the offerings made in the temple, to contribute wood for the altar, to give their first fruits and their firstborn to the Lord, and to tithe. They promised to live as the people of God and take good care of the place where God dwelled among them. To move from confession to this level of commitment inspires me. It's the spirit of repentance.

Unfortunately, the people didn't fully uphold their commitment. When Nehemiah returned to Babylon, things started to unravel in Jerusalem. Upon his return to Judah, he found the people desecrating the Sabbath (Nehemiah 13:17). He warned them that they were falling into the same patterns that had gotten their ancestors in trouble. I get it. Change is not easy. It's difficult to undo bad habits or relearn new ones. That's true for spiritual practices as well as our work patterns. But we can commit to work differently.

I've been paying close attention to my tendency to overwork so that I do it less. With the help of therapists and my spiritual director, I've learned that I have very high expectations for myself. No one else holds me to the same standards. Even though I'm long out of school, I still want to do A-level work, earning the highest marks on every task. Some of the best advice I ever received was that I could turn in B-level work occasionally. What that means is that I don't always have to strive for perfection. Not every task demands my best effort. Sometimes good is good enough.

I also have to watch out for impostor syndrome. Impostor syndrome is the persistent belief that we're actually not that intelligent, competent, or skillful even though evidence to the contrary exists. Those with impostor syndrome can feel paralyzing doubt about their abilities. When my impostor syndrome creeps up, I'm prone to work really hard to prove that I belong and that I can hack it while I'm drowning in doubt and insecurity on the inside. All of that overwork is a recipe for exhaustion and all other sorts of stress-related issues. It doesn't serve me, my team, or my organization. So I need to cast it aside and choose to work differently.

Remember Tom the appraiser? He didn't let the mistake he made early in his career define him. Instead, he let it refine and redefine him. In his work, he always strove to be honest, but this incident made being ethical a core value in his life. It also brought a new compassion and empathy for those who make both little and big mistakes. Now, as a successful business owner in the real estate industry, he not only strives to be ethical in all of his dealings, he even teaches aspiring professionals to be ethical in their work.

Our mistakes and missteps don't have to define us either. Rather we can leverage what we've learned to approach our work in healthier ways. We can start to remove ourselves from the work hurt equation. Instead of being part of the problem, we can take initiative in areas where we need to grow and become part of the solution.

WORK HURT CLINIC

History: To what extent could you have contributed to your work hurt? Place a check next to any that you have experienced or are currently experiencing.

- Made an error or mistake at work
- Violated a protocol or policy
- Spoke or acted in a way that was inconsistent with the organization's values or my profession's ethics
- Failed to communicate about my needs, goals, and expectations
- Neglected to communicate about when and why I've felt frustrated, underappreciated, or overworked
- Not communicated with kindness, honesty, humility, and self-control
- Done more work than is required for a task
- Struggled to prioritize tasks and manage my workload
- Not spent adequate time resting and playing
- Little to no excitement about my work
- Poor fit between my skills and training and my job
- Poor fit between my values and my organization's values

Care:
- Tell the truth.
- Find your fit, if possible.
- Commit to work differently.

Remembering to Hope

WHERE IS THE TRAIL? I started to panic. My family and I were deep in the forest at Pictured Rocks National Lakeshore, and I wasn't sure we would find our way out. Somehow, we had veered off the main trail on our hike, and I couldn't see any markers or hear any people nearby to guide us back. I quickly pulled out my phone to open Google Maps only to realize we had no cellular service. Thankfully the GPS tracker on my phone worked, and I could see a pulsing blue dot on the map indicating our location, but without cellular service, I couldn't chart a clear course to the parking lot. I had to rely on our position, our bearing, and my vague memory of the path that got us there to get home. But all the trees looked the same. Every clearing looked like a path. We were lost.

To be without hope is to feel truly lost. That's precisely where we can find ourselves in the wake of work hurt regardless of the role we played in it. It's disorienting and can make us feel completely out of place. But hope still exists, we just need to know where to look for it. We need a little help remembering God's steadfast love and faithfulness so that we can take courage in the darkest moments.

HOPE IS HARD TO SEE

After college, Marc worked as an accountant for several years. Over time, he sensed a call to make a change. That change required more training, so he enrolled in graduate school. While in school, he was offered a job leading a prominent institute within the university. This institute functioned like a nonprofit. Faculty members affiliated with the institute conducted research that was intended to serve a wide audience beyond the university. During his time as the institute's director, Marc helped expand the institute's influence through his administrative sophistication and organizational leadership.

One day, Marc's supervisor told him he couldn't remain in his job because he didn't have the right credentials and affiliations. Typically institutes were led by people who had earned a doctorate. Marc was working on his, but having a doctorate or the specific affiliations weren't required when they offered him the job, and they weren't a stipulation in his keeping it. Still, after almost a decade in the role, he was terminated under the guise he wasn't qualified.

Marc had been deceived. He learned from a friend that he was actually let go because the school had financial troubles and chose to eliminate Marc's position to save money. Marc also realized that he was just another casualty of a school president who had been firing people abruptly and without cause. He even recalled that another colleague who was let go without cause had to seek counseling to help her process that trauma.

I asked Marc if he considered bringing a wrongful termination suit against the university, but he said he didn't know his options at the time. His job was "at-will," meaning, in part, that the school could "terminate an employee at any time for any reason, except an illegal one, or for no reason without incurring legal liability."[1] Plus, he felt powerless to do anything because he was a Black man working in a predominately White institution. What was particularly egregious and hurtful to Marc was that this was a Christian university charged with training the next generation of leaders. I asked Marc how he remained hopeful in the midst of such a terrible situation. His termination came out of nowhere and blindsided him. He replied, "Hope is hard to see while you're in it."

RETRACING OUR STEPS

In deep valleys and dark moments, finding hope is difficult but not impossible. Let's look at Jeremiah's story as an example. When the walls fell down around Jerusalem, Jeremiah lamented. He shared his griefs and frustrations with God. He explained the depth of his anguish and the height of his hope. Lamentations 3 is perhaps the most familiar lament Jeremiah recorded. It's a bit different from the first two, which focus on the destruction of Jerusalem. In this one, Jeremiah emphasized his personal pain. He began, "I am the man who has seen affliction by the rod of the LORD's wrath." It's a poem of misery. By the time we get to Lamentations 3:19-20, we're ready to take Jeremiah at his word:

> I remember my affliction and my wandering,
>   the bitterness and the gall.
> I well remember them,
>   and my soul is downcast within me.
>   (Lamentations 3:19-20)

My soul would be downcast too—maybe worse. But Jeremiah didn't ruminate on his misery. Instead, he recalled the Lord's faithful love. To me, it's one of the most profound "dig deep" moments in all of Scripture. In the midst of his pain, Jeremiah found hope through remembering. He said,

> Yet this I call to mind
> and therefore I have hope. (Lamentations 3:21)

We'll unpack the "this" in a bit. For now, we're just going to marvel that someone in the throes of despair found hope.

Hope is more than wishful thinking. Hope is believing and watching for God to fulfill his promises. It is future oriented. And we're seeing ourselves as part of that future. Hope is expecting that, by the power of the Spirit, God will continue to be present with us and working to redeem, reconcile, and restore what is broken in our world, and that, when Jesus returns, he will make all things new. A close examination of hope in the Bible reveals that our ability to hope is connected to our convictions about what God has done and will do to keep his promises. While being future focused, it's anchored in what we know God has done in the past.

During my doctoral studies, I examined biblical hope alongside neuroscience and cognitive psychology. I came upon something called episodic future thinking (EFT), which is our ability to imagine ourselves in the future. We engage in EFT all the time—when we think about what we'll have for dinner, where we'll go on vacation, and where we'd like to be in our careers in five years. I discovered that hope has a lot in common with EFT.

> *A close examination of hope in the Bible reveals that our ability to hope is connected to our convictions about what God has done and will do to keep his promises.*

Researchers believe our ability to imagine ourselves in the future relies on our memories. Through brain scans, they've observed that thinking about the future stimulates areas of the brain where we store memories. So they believe that when we're thinking about the future, our brains are actually re-membering—putting together the pieces of our past to imagine new situations. Curt Thompson explains it slightly differently, "Your memory creates your future. That's because you imagine the future through the neural networks created by your past."² But the point is the same: the past is vital to how we envision the future; remembering is essential to hope.

But the key is *what* we're remembering. Sometimes, when I'm thinking about the future, my brain likes to remember painful or difficult situations. Instead of hope, I end up with anxiety and dread. But, with God's help, my mind can piece together other stories—the stories of when things have gone well and when I've experienced God's provision and care. That's when I experience hope.

Now we can get back to what Jeremiah remembered and how it helped him find hope in the wake of grief. Jeremiah prayed,

> Because of the LORD's great love we are not consumed,
>   for his compassions never fail.
> They are new every morning;
>   great is your faithfulness. (Lamentations 3:22-23)

He continued by listing many reasons he could have hope in God. And in Lamentations 3:31-33 he declared,

> For no one is cast off
>   by the Lord forever.
> Though he brings grief, he will show compassion,
>   so great is his unfailing love.
> For he does not willingly bring affliction
>   or grief to anyone.

Jeremiah remembered what he knew to be true about God. Specifically, he recalled God acting in congruence with his character. The words *never fail* and *faithfulness* describe God's actions. And the words *great love, compassion,* and *unfailing love* speak to his character.

What the NIV translates as "great love" and "unfailing love" is the Hebrew word *hesed*, which means God's loyal or steadfast covenant love. In *The Jesus Storybook Bible*, Sally Lloyd-Jones calls it "God's Never Stopping, Never Giving Up, Unbreaking, Always and Forever

Love."[3] The word *compassion* is the Hebrew word *rakham*. Both *hesed* and *rakham* figure prominently in the name of God revealed to Moses: "The LORD, the LORD, the compassionate and gracious God, slow to anger, abounding in love and faithfulness, maintaining love to thousands" (Exodus 34:6-7). As he recalled the Lord's love and compassion, Jeremiah knew that the only proper response was to address the sin and rebellion that brought on the destruction of Jerusalem. He exhorted,

> Let us examine our ways and test them,
>   and let us return to the LORD.
> Let us lift up our hearts and our hands
>   to God in heaven, and say:
> "We have sinned and rebelled
>   and you have not forgiven.
>
> "You have covered yourself with anger and pursued us;
>   you have slain us without pity. . . .
> You have made us scum and refuse
>   among the nations." (Lamentations 3:40-43, 45)

Still confident in the goodness of God, Jeremiah could ask God to take vengeance on Judah's enemies: "Pay them back what they deserve, LORD, for what their hands have done" (Lamentations 3:64). Jeremiah called to mind the steadfast love of the Lord and the fact that God's mercies are new every morning. He held on to this and therefore he had hope.

FOLLOWING THE TRAIL

Jeremiah wasn't the only one to recall the lovingkindness of God in the wake of Jerusalem's destruction. Both Ezra and Nehemiah initiated the work of rebuilding the city because of the hope they had in God. Recalling God's steadfast love and faithfulness helped the Israelites return home and commit to the work of rebuilding and restoring what had been broken. Evidence of God's loyal love is sprinkled throughout Ezra and Nehemiah and the return-to-Jerusalem narrative.

First, God moved the heart of Cyrus to rebuild the temple in Jerusalem and to release the captives to do the work (Ezra 1:1-4). The return trip was fraught with potential danger. Even when the Israelites returned to Jerusalem and began work on the temple, leaders in the Trans-Euphrates attempted to thwart their efforts. Yet God was with them. The book of Ezra records, "But the eye of their God was watching over the elders of the Jews, and they were not stopped until a report could go to Darius and his written reply received" (Ezra 5:5). When the foundation of the temple had been laid, God's people celebrated with joy. The priests and the Levites sang a familiar refrain to the Lord: "He is good; his love toward Israel endures forever" (Ezra 3:11). Ezra the priest didn't arrive in Jerusalem until after the work on the temple had started. He attributed the speed of his journey from Babylon to Jerusalem to the fact that "the gracious hand of God was on him" (Ezra 7:9). Ezra believed that the favor he had with King Artaxerxes was because of God's loyal love. Ezra said,

> Praise be to the LORD, the God of our ancestors, who has put it into the king's heart to bring honor to the house of the LORD in Jerusalem in this way and who has extended his good favor to me before the king and his advisers and all the king's powerful officials. Because the hand of the LORD my God was on me, I took courage and gathered leaders from Israel to go up with me. (Ezra 7:27-28)

What the NIV translates as "good favor" is actually *hesed*. Ezra experienced God's loyal love in the form of moving the heart of a king, and he noted that the hand of God was on him. Remembering God's care for him brought him courage.

Ezra was keenly aware of how God's steadfast love had preserved and provided for the Israelites. When he arrived in Jerusalem, he discovered that many of the people and their leaders had married people outside of their Jewish faith, which God had forbidden (Deuteronomy 7:3). Ezra was distraught. Yet even in the midst of his prayer of confession, he professed, "[God] has shown us kindness in the sight of the kings of Persia: He has granted us new life to rebuild the house of our God and repair its ruins, and he has given us a wall of protection in Judah and Jerusalem" (Ezra 9:8-9). The word translated "kindness" is *hesed*. In a moment of profound discouragement, Ezra focused his attention on what God had done for his people.

Nehemiah called on the God of loyal love to grant him favor with King Artaxerxes. God did. When Sanballat and Tobiah were ridiculing the people and threatening the work on the wall, Nehemiah gave the people hope by charging them to recall the character and consistency of God. "Don't be afraid of them," he said. "Remember the Lord, who is great and awesome, and fight for your families, your sons and your daughters, your wives and your homes" (Nehemiah 4:14). Without a doubt, God was orchestrating this magnificent work of rebuilding. In the end, everyone—including the enemies of God who tried to thwart the rebuilding—could see God's hand in all of it.

In their prayer of confession, the people recalled the marvelous acts of God on behalf of his covenant people. Looking back to the destruction of Jerusalem and the exile, they said to God, "But in your great mercy you did not put an end to them or abandon them, for you are a gracious and merciful God" (Nehemiah 9:31). Then before bringing their petition before God, they proclaimed his character again: "Now therefore, our God, the great God, mighty and awesome, who keeps his covenant of love. . . . In all that has happened to us, you have remained righteous; you have acted faithfully, while we have acted wickedly" (Nehemiah 9:32-33). In these verses, the words for "mercy" and "merciful" are *rakham*, the word that means compassion, and "covenant of love" is actually "covenant of *hesed*."

With all that had gone wrong—from the destruction of Jerusalem to the daunting task of rebuilding the city's temples and wall—God's people maintained the hope that God would continue to work on their behalf because of the ways he consistently demonstrated his compassion and love toward his people throughout history. The ability to recount the faithfulness of God helped the people get the work done. It also fueled their celebration and worship when it was complete. When they dedicated the temple, they rejoiced. The Scriptures tell us, "And on that day they offered great sacrifices, rejoicing because God had given them great joy. The women and children also rejoiced. The sound of rejoicing in Jerusalem could be heard far away" (Nehemiah 12:43).

HOW TO FIND THE TRAIL

Hope isn't easy, especially in the messy middle of work hurt. Loss, hardship, and suffering make difficult to trust that God still loves us and is working for our good and for his glory. Yet we can find hope in the wake of our hurt; Marc did. Two practices helped Marc discover hope in the darkness.

Remembering God's faithfulness in our lives. First, Marc remembered how God had provided for him in the past. Marc could rely on his memory to a degree, but he also referred to his journal. In his journal he had recorded not only what he learned from the Scriptures but also how he experienced God's love and care in his life. Marc could identify specific instances in the past in which God had come through for him in a tough situation. The past faithfulness of God gave Marc hope that God could provide again. Remembering acts of God's past faithfulness helped Marc find his way back to hope.

Remembering can give us the courage to keep going, believing that God has a bright future in store for us. The ancient Israelites would set up stones of remembrance as a reminder of all that God had done for them. We could do something similar, writing an act of God's faithfulness on a small river rock or a piece of paper and storing the collection in a jar on the counter. Or we could write in a journal and review it like Marc did. Journaling doesn't require a leather-bound diary and fancy pen. It doesn't have to take a lot of time either. We can start simply by recording three good things that happened during the course of each day or three things we're thankful for.[4] Over time, in those lists we can discern the presence and provision of God. Finally, we can also rehearse the ways we've experienced God's loyal love and faithfulness with our friends and family and in our worship services. The act of sharing reinforces the events in our memories, and our memories contribute to our ability to hope.

Remembering the Scriptures. Second, Marc took comfort in the Scriptures. The Bible tells one big story that is comprised of hundreds of smaller stories of God's faithfulness. Immersing ourselves in those stories and in the passages that proclaim and demonstrate God's character floods our heads and hearts with evidence of God's faithfulness and lovingkindness. When we dwell on the Scriptures—read them, listen to them, retell them, we get the stories of God's good works into our minds so that they're available to be remembered when it's time to exercise hope.

REMEMBERING THAT GOD IS AT WORK

We, too, can recall the Lord's lovingkindness and compassion in the wake of work hurt. When I interviewed Marc to hear his story, he didn't start at the beginning. Rather he started at the end. He believed that his work hurt ultimately propelled him to where God designed him to be—not running another institute or directing a program for a nonprofit but rather teaching in higher education. He got a job doing precisely that within a few months of being terminated at his other job. He took other jobs here and there and unfortunately experienced work hurt in many of them. Now he's teaching once again and absolutely loves it. And he can follow the trail all the way back to when he was fired from that job and beyond. He can trace God's loyal love and faithfulness. That's the source of his hope.

After hearing Marc's story, I recalled the story of Joseph, who said to his brothers after they reunited, "You intended to harm me, but God intended it for good to accomplish what is now being done, the saving of many lives" (Genesis 50:20). To maintain hope in bleak circumstances, we've got to remember God's character and consistency—his compassion, love, and faithfulness—and be on the lookout for evidence that God is at work.

> *To maintain hope in bleak circumstances, we've got to remember God's character and consistency—his compassion, love, and faithfulness—and be on the lookout for evidence that God is at work.*

Marc told me that hope can be opaque. "It's hard to see while you're in it, but God gives you cameos." God shows up in brief, sometimes unexpected ways, but we can miss them if we're not watchful. We need to be on the lookout for God's watchful eye and strong hand accompanying us when we're in the deep, dark valleys of work hurt. God was with us when work beat us up and broke our hearts. He didn't turn his face away or ignore our pain. And he's still with us as we try to pick up the pieces. We need to pay attention because God is at work, often behind the scenes helping us rebuild, even when we cannot see.

WORK HURT CLINIC

Symptoms: Which is the most difficult for you in the wake of work hurt?

- Finding hope
- Finding your way
- Remembering God's love

Care:

- Remember God's faithfulness in your life.
- Remember the Scriptures.

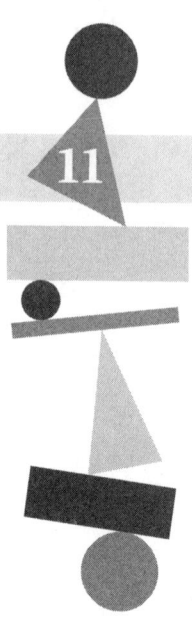

11

Working in the New Jerusalem

THE STATE OF MICHIGAN HAS 129 lighthouses. Some sit atop a rocky coast or back from the water's edge. Others rest on piers or jetties that jut out from the shoreline. The Big Sable Point Lighthouse on the shore of Lake Michigan is just a few steps above a sandy beach. On a gorgeous May morning, I hiked out to it, toured the keeper's quarters, and climbed the steps to the top of the tower. Then I followed the shoreline back to the parking lot. The weather was perfect—blue skies, light breeze, waves gently lapping the shore. In the middle of a beautiful day, it's easy to forget why the lighthouses were built in the first place. A storm helps you remember.

I'll never forget our family's visit to the Au Sable Light Station on Lake Superior. The wind whipped our faces as we walked through the cedar forest to Au Sable Point. The lake roared. There were whitecaps as far as we could see. The lighthouse grounds sat atop a rocky cliff. We strolled about, taking in the sights as we waited for our tour. At one point, as I leaned down to take a photograph of some wildflowers, a wave crashed below me, the spray splashing up and over me. Startled, I backed away from the cliff's edge. Seeing the violent waters made me realize how necessary the lighthouse was. Day or night it could offer a beam of hope to a ship caught in a storm.

We all know people who have experienced work hurt. In a span of one month, five of my friends lost their jobs. When I asked people to tell me a work hurt story for this book, several of them asked me, "Which one?" So many people experience work as painful labor. It's thorns and thistles, toil and trouble. It breaks their bodies and their hearts. They can scarcely imagine that God created work to be good. But what if our lives—our resilience—can tell them a different story about work? What if we can be a light to someone else who's sitting in the darkness?

> *What if we can be a light to someone else who's sitting in the darkness?*

THE NEW JERUSALEM

A word of the Lord spoken through the prophet Zechariah gives us a glimpse of how this is possible. Alongside Haggai, Zechariah ministered to the exiles who had returned to rebuild the temple. A group of people, newly arrived home from Babylon, asked Zechariah if their religious practices—like fasting—should look the same now as they had in the past. Zechariah didn't give them a straight answer. Instead, the Lord spoke through Zechariah: *Is that what you call fasting?* The Lord had told their ancestors, "Administer true justice; show mercy and compassion to one another. Do not oppress the widow or the fatherless, the foreigner or the poor. Do not plot evil against each other" (Zechariah 7:9). Time and again God told his people that their religious rituals were meaningless apart from righteousness and everyday faithfulness. But they wouldn't listen, and so the Lord "scattered them with a whirlwind among the nations, where they were strangers" (Zechariah 7:14). Destruction and exile were their punishment.

Yet God didn't dwell on the past and Israel's unceasing unfaithfulness. Instead, he looked toward the future. He gave them a vision of what could be. *Picture this: You're old and gray, enjoying watching your children's children play in the streets. The harvest will be plentiful. The wine will be sweet. I will dwell with you, and you, my people, will be a blessing to the nations.*

God wanted this for his people, but they had a role to play. They had to participate with him in building this future. First, they had to restore their city. God told them, "Let your hands be strong so that the temple may be built" (Zechariah 8:9). He gave them physical labor to do. But he also gave them the job of loving their neighbor well. "Speak the truth to each other," he commanded, "and render true and sound judgment in your courts; do not plot evil against your neighbor, and do not love to swear falsely. I hate all this" (Zechariah 8:16-17). As he had with their ancestors, God wanted this people to pursue righteousness, justice, and mercy. As had been God's hope from the beginning, his people's faithfulness would make them a light to the nations.

God gave the people a glimpse at how their everyday faithfulness could pay off. They could complete the temple and rebuild the wall. Peace and goodness could overcome the strife and discord in their life together. Their once desolate land could be fruitful again, and their worship could be filled with joy (Zechariah 8:19). That would cause the people of the earth to take notice. People from the surrounding cities would see something distinctive about the people of God. The nations would see God's people returning to their ruined city, determined to rebuild it brick by brick. They would observe their everyday faithfulness and the undeniable presence of God in their midst. And the people of the nations would want a taste of that for themselves. They would come to Jerusalem to seek the living and loving God.

The implications of their faithfulness would reach far beyond the walls of Jerusalem. God said through Zechariah, "In those days ten men from all languages and nations will take firm hold of one Jew by the hem of his robe and say, 'Let us go with you, because we have heard that God is with you'" (Zechariah 8:23). Through Zechariah, the Lord gave this beautiful picture of the far-reaching ramifications of resilient people living in righteousness. The Lord's fame would multiply tenfold because of their faithfulness.

When the walls fell down and they were carried off into exile, the Israelites could have remained in their grief. They could have opted for a different sort of life far away from home and far away from God. Yet God had a plan for the remnant who would return. Isaiah prophesied,

> Your people will rebuild the ancient ruins
> and will raise up the age-old foundations;
> You will be called Repairer of Broken Walls,
> Restorer of Streets with Dwellings. (Isaiah 58:12)

They would once again flourish in the land, and they would find their joy in God (Isaiah 58:14).

When work beats us up, burns us out, or breaks our hearts, we also have a choice. We can flame out or rekindle our fire. Consistent with God's plan for his people to be a light to the nations, Jesus told his followers to be the light of the world. We can't be the light of the world when we're overcome with work hurt. Left untended, the pain caused by our work hurt can eat away at us, seep out onto others, and make our light grow dim. Yet Jesus doesn't call us to be a flicker. He calls us to be a flame—a beacon to the weary and broken, illuminating the way to him.

LIGHT FOR CHRIS

Toward the end of college, Chris envisioned himself working with the critically ill—perhaps in emergency services or in a healthcare setting. He wasn't sure what direction to take, but he was certain that he wanted to get far away from his turbulent homelife. After graduating, he moved across the country to a big city where one of his closest friends had already taken a job.

Initially, he got a minimum wage position in a hospital and began taking some classes he needed to get into nursing school. He later took a job at a small, local fire department. He did well in that job and loved the work. It confirmed his love for emergency services. Eventually Chris got into an accelerated nurse practitioner program. Within a year he got his nursing license and met his wife. The future seemed bright, and Chris felt invincible.

Then the pandemic hit. Nursing students weren't allowed to be in hospitals or interact with patients. His program went completely online, and he recalled how discussion boards devolved into venting sessions—and not just about school. He felt disillusioned; this wasn't what he had signed up for. Since he already had his nursing license, he decided to drop out of the program and get a job.

Chris went to work at a large municipal fire department. Even though he had previously worked as a firefighter, all new hires had to participate in a six-month training academy. The first six weeks were brutal. Trainees had to take an EMT (emergency medical technician) course. It was really difficult, but since he had previously received EMT training, Chris tutored his classmates. Still, six of them failed. Chris recalls being in his perfectly pressed uniform and having to march around the one-mile training ground track while those who failed the course were called in one-by-one to be fired. Meanwhile the instructor marched next to the rest of the class making sure they knew those recruits were being terminated. He told them, "People are having their careers ended right this second." Chris told me it was so stressful and intense. It made him realize that he was in a toxic work environment.

Chris graduated the academy in good standing. He then had to complete a probationary period in a firehouse. Each shift, he had a set of tasks and drills he had to complete under a supervising officer called a drill instructor. Enter Frank. Chris described Frank as a drill sergeant—demanding and harsh. He kept Chris up late into the night, pelting him with questions. He intentionally tested Chris on topics he said Chris didn't need to know for a particular shift. He lured Chris into a false sense of security, assuring him that little mistakes wouldn't be a big deal. Then he would write Chris up at the end of a shift, sometimes citing the most minor of infractions on what was an otherwise exemplary day of work for Chris. Chris felt like he had no power to dissent. If he argued or pushed back, he feared Frank would report him for having a poor attitude. Chris felt like Frank was looking for him to fail.

During this time, Chris's fire station had an unusually high call volume. In the height of the pandemic, they were responding to shootings, stabbings, sexual assault, rape, domestic violence, and drug abuse situations. The intensity of that work compounded the stress Chris was already feeling from Frank and the unforgiving culture he created in the firehouse.

Chris met with a union representative who told Chris his job was in trouble—he could be fired. This worried Chris considerably since his wife was pregnant with their first child. He began vomiting daily before work and shaking when he arrived at the firehouse. The anxiety and stress were so overwhelming that Chris needed medication. He even filed a complaint with the city—hoping for someone to intervene on his behalf—but nothing happened.

When his time at Frank's station concluded, Chris went to another station to complete his probationary period. There he had another drill instructor who was very strict but also very fair, according to Chris. Chris did really well at this new station. His first eight shifts went perfectly, but he had one drill that went poorly. He told me that's normal during the probationary period. Sometimes you have a bad drill. But because of all of his history with Frank, that one poor drill had terrible consequences. Chris was brought before the Probationary Committee, who gave him a warning—one more mistake, one more bad drill, and he was done. Chris had no room for error. So when he made a mistake a few shifts later, he was fired. He couldn't believe it.

Chris remembers how difficult it was to tell his father-in-law that he had been let go from his job. He had a wife, a baby girl, and no job. Instead of disappointment, Chris received love: "He said that he believed in me and that he trusted me with his daughter and granddaughter. . . . He was able to walk with me through that in a unique manner." Chris's father-in-law could show him compassion and empathy because he had been there before. We've actually already met Chris's father-in-law earlier in this book. Chris's father-in-law is Tom, the real estate appraiser who was fired for making a mistake. He, too, had to come home without a job to a wife and a baby girl. Tom and his wife had another daughter a few years later. They named her Lindsey. Lindsey grew up, and she married Chris.

Tom's work hurt was profound, and he has to relive it every time an attorney seeks to attack his character and competence by bringing up the mistake that cost him his job. Still, with God's help, he has overcome his pain. He's become resilient. So now he can not only withstand the character attacks while keeping his integrity intact, he can show compassion and empathy to others in similar situations.

And Chris can look back and tell the story of how God cared for him in wake of his work hurt. God loved Chris through Tom and through the provision of a new job. After Chris was fired, he immediately started applying for nursing jobs. Thank God for that nursing license. He got three interviews and had a job offer within two weeks. He told me, "This is what shows that God is faithful." He shared, "I would have been in a much darker place. I'm now able to recognize God for that. I felt caught. I felt taken care of in that moment. I remember driving home and thinking, 'Thank you, Jesus, for my nursing license. I'm going to be able to feed my kid.'"

HEALING ON THE OTHER SIDE OF HURT

With God's help, we can move from the ash heap and rubble of our work hurt to become rebuilders, renewers, repairers, and restorers in this broken world. Like Tom, Luis learned that healing exists on the other side of the hurt. He experienced upward bullying while working as a college administrator. One of his direct reports, someone who had been his friend and colleague, made his life miserable. Now Luis works in a different field in a job that's also a good fit for him and a good pace. He misses working in higher education and hopes to get back to it at some point. For now, he's pursuing contentment. He feels stronger than he ever did. And he feels healed. He told me that he learned a lot in the midst of his work hurt. James, he said, talks about the testing of your faith: "Consider it pure joy, my brothers and sisters, whenever you face trials of many kinds, because you know that the testing of your faith produces perseverance" (James 1:2-3).

James continues, "Let perseverance finish its work so that you may be mature and complete, not lacking anything" (James 1:4). Apparently, perseverance has needed to do a lot of work on me. Even though I've mostly healed from much of my own work hurt, work still threatens to beat me up, burn me out, and break my heart. In both my paid and unpaid work, I find reasons to raise my fists in the air, shout into the void, and even cry. When that happens, I go back to many of the practices I've described in this book. I'll scribble a lament in my journal, listen to a playlist that reminds me of God's lovingkindness, study a section of Scripture to discern what obedience looks like in that particular situation, and seek support

> *Let perseverance finish its work so that you may be mature and complete, not lacking anything.*
> **JAMES 1:4**

from loving people in my community. Those practices help me build resilience. They create within me an inner strength that helps me withstand the blows a little better each time work tries to knock me down.

FROM DARKNESS TO LIGHT

Work hurt can shove us into deep, dark valleys because it's disorienting, embarrassing, and isolating. But that displacement we experience can be the prime arena for discernment. It can be a time of earnestly listening to our lives and paying attention to the stirrings in our hearts. We can commit ourselves to everyday faithfulness—loving God and neighbor with the gifts, talents, and resources God has entrusted to us. We can courageously take our next most faithful step—even if that's getting out of bed and scrolling through job listings. Resolving to get up out of the rubble in the wake of work hurt builds resilience. We need to be resilient because work can continue to disappoint, disillusion, and even devastate us until Jesus comes back.

Through our resilience, we can reflect God's light in a dark world. Through our everyday faithfulness, we can point others to our faithful God. Work hurt cannot have the final word. That alone belongs to God, who is writing our story. And in his last chapter, thorns and thistles will have no sting. In the new Jerusalem—the one yet to come—work can't beat us up, burn us out, or break our hearts. Painful labor will be a fleeting memory. Troublesome toil will be no more. And we will work with unending joy.

Acknowledgments

THIS BOOK WOULD NOT BE POSSIBLE without the amazing people who stood beside me and helped me write this book, page by page. Ruth Buchanan, you helped me extract this book from my head and my heart and rooted for me every step of the way. You're an extraordinary writing coach, and I'm glad to call you my friend. Keely Boeving of WordServe Literary, you've supported me and this book from the first day we met. I'm lucky to have you as my agent. Al Hsu and the team at InterVarsity Press, your vision for this book inspired me to keep writing on the days when I felt I had no words left. Thanks for shaping this offering into something beautiful.

So many friends, coworkers, and students have encouraged me and prayed for me while I wrote and revised. They reminded me time and again that this book matters. Thanks especially to the De Pree Center team for your steadfast support and enthusiasm.

Last, but not least, this book would not be possible without the support of my family. Mom, Dad, Lissy, Aunt Val, and Dada, I'm so lucky to be loved by each of you. To Neal, Jeremiah, and Caleb, you sacrificed the most for me to write this book. But you've also been my biggest cheerleaders. I love you all, and I hope that this book and my work in the world helps you to experience less work hurt in yours.

Notes

INTRODUCTION: THE PAIN OF WORK

[1] Evan Cunningham, "Great Recession, Great Recovery? Trends from the Current Population Survey," *Monthly Labor Review*, U.S. Bureau of Labor Statistics, April 2018, https://doi.org/10.21916/mlr.2018.10.

[2] United Nations Department of Economic and Social Affairs, "The Sustainable Development Goals Report 2021, Goal 8: Decent Work and Economic Growth," unstats.un.org, 2021, https://unstats.un.org/sdgs/report/2021/goal-08/.

[3] Georgetown University Center on Education and the Workforce, "Tracking COVID-19 Unemployment and Job Losses," cew.georgetown,edu, 2024, https://cew.georgetown.edu/cew-reports/jobtracker/.

[4] See the U.S. Bureau of Labor Statistics, Job Openings and Labor Turnover Survey, number of quits, total non-farm, seasonally adjusted, accessed June 8, 2023, https://www.bls.gov/data/home.htm.

[5] See U.S. Bureau of Labor Statistics, Job Openings and Labor Turnover Survey, number of layoffs, total non-farm, seasonally adjusted, June 8, 2023, https://www.bls.gov/data/home.htm.

[6] McKinsey & Company, "What Is Burnout?" August 14, 2023, www.mckinsey.com/featured-insights/mckinsey-explainers/what-is-burnout.

[7] E. Beth Hemphill, "Uncomfortable (but Necessary) Conversations About Burnout," *Gallup* (blog), December 6, 2022, www.gallup.com/workplace/406232/uncomfortable-necessary-conversations-burnout.aspx.

[8] Gallup. "How to Prevent Employee Burnout," 2024, www.gallup.com/workplace/313160/preventing-and-dealing-with-employee-burnout.aspx; Jen Fisher, "Workplace Burnout Survey: Burnout Without Borders," Deloitte, 2024, www2.deloitte.com/us/en/pages/about-deloitte/articles/burnout-survey.html.

⁹Ben Wigert, "Employee Burnout: The Biggest Myth," *Gallup* (blog), March 13, 2020, www.gallup.com/workplace/288539/employee-burnout-biggest-myth.aspx.

¹⁰Stephanie Marken and Sangeeta Agrawal, "K-12 Workers Have Highest Burnout Rate in U.S.," *Gallup* (blog), June 13, 2022, https://news.gallup.com/poll/393500/workers-highest-burnout-rate.aspx.

¹¹International Labour Organization and Lloyd's Register Foundation, "Experiences of Violence and Harassment at Work: A Global First Survey," International Labour Organization, December 2, 2022, www.ilo.org/publications/major-publications/experiences-violence-and-harassment-work-global-first-survey.

¹²UC San Diego Center on Gender Equity and Health and Stop Street Harassment, "Measuring #MeToo: A National Study on Sexual Harassment and Assault," Stopstreetharassment.org, April 2019, www.stopstreetharassment.org/wp-content/uploads/2012/08/2019-MeToo-National-Sexual-Harassment-and-Assault-Report.pdf.

¹³Kenneth Terrell, "Age Discrimination Common in Workplace, Survey Says," AARP, August 2, 2018, www.aarp.org/work/age-discrimination/common-at-work/.

¹⁴Gallup, "Employee Engagement," Gallup Indicators, 2024, www.gallup.com/394373/indicator-employee-engagement.aspx.

¹⁵Sarah Jaffe, *Work Won't Love You Back: How Devotion to Our Jobs Keeps Us Exploited, Exhausted, and Alone* (New York: Bold Type Books, 2021).

¹⁶C. Meyer, "עָצַב," in Theological Dictionary of the Old Testament, ed. G. Johannes Botterweck, Helmer Ringgren, and Heinz-Josef Fabry, trans. John T. Willis, Douglas W. Stott, and David E. Green (Grand Rapids, MI: Eerdmans, 1978), 3:278-80.

¹⁷Brené Brown, *Dare to Lead: Brave Work. Tough Conversations. Whole Hearts* (New York: Random House, 2018), 85.

¹⁸Steven Garber, *Visions of Vocation: Common Grace for the Common Good* (Downers Grove, IL: InterVarsity Press, 2014).

¹⁹Richard Rohr, "Transforming Pain," *Center for Action and Contemplation* (blog), October 17, 2018, https://cac.org/daily-meditations/transforming-pain-2018-10-17/.

²⁰J. J. Cutuli and Ann S. Masten, "Resilience," in *The Encyclopedia of Positive Psychology*, ed. Shane J. Lopez (New York: Wiley, 2009), 837-43.

1. WHEN THE WALLS FALL DOWN

[1] Nicole F. Roberts, "Emotional & Physical Pain Are Almost the Same—To Your Brain," *Forbes.com*, February 14, 2020, www.forbes.com/sites/nicole fisher/2020/02/14/emotional--physical-pain-are-almost-the-sameto-your-brain/.

[2] You can view the 2019 Indeed commercial at www.popisms.com/Television Commercial/211533/Indeed-Commercial-Promotion-Indeed-US-2019.

[3] Maury Gittleman, "The 'Great Resignation' in Perspective," *Monthly Labor Review*, U.S. Bureau of Labor Statistics, July 2022, https://doi.org/10.21916/mlr.2022.20.

[4] Kim Parker and Juliana Menasce Horowitz, "Majority of Workers Who Quit a Job in 2021 Cite Low Pay, No Opportunities for Advancement, Feeling Disrespected," *Pew Research Center* (blog), March 9, 2022, www.pewresearch.org/fact-tank/2022/03/09/majority-of-workers-who-quit-a-job-in-2021-cite-low-pay-no-opportunities-for-advancement-feeling-disrespected/.

[5] *Merriam-Webster.com Dictionary*, s.v. "devastate," accessed July 1, 2024, www.merriam-webster.com/dictionary/devastate.

[6] PYMNTS, "Banks Slash 60K Jobs as Dealmaking and IPOs Decline," December 26, 2023, www.pymnts.com/news/banking/2023/banks-slash-60k-jobs-as-dealmaking-and-ipos-decline/.

[7] Walter A. Elwell and Barry J. Beitzel, "Tabernacle, Temple," in *Baker Encyclopedia of the Bible* (Grand Rapids, MI: Baker Books, 1988), 2015-29.

[8] C. E. Shepherd, s.v. "Jerusalem," in *The Lexham Bible Dictionary*, ed. John D. Barry, Lexham Bible Reference Series (Bellingham, WA: Lexham Press, 2016).

[9] Shepherd, s.v. "Jerusalem."

[10] John Monson, "Solomon's Temple," in *Dictionary of the Old Testament: Historical Books*, ed. Bill T. Arnold and H. G. M. Williamson (Downers Grove, IL: IVP Academic, 2005), 929.

[11] Vasundhara Sawhney, "Managing Difficult Emotions at Work: Our Favorite Reads," *HBR Ascend*, March 22, 2022, https://hbr.org/2022/03/managing-difficult-emotions-at-work-our-favorite-reads.

[12] World Health Organization, "Burn-out an 'Occupational Phenomenon': International Classification of Diseases," *World Health Organization News* (blog), May 28, 2019, www.who.int/news/item/28-05-2019-burn-out-an-occupational-phenomenon-international-classification-of-diseases.

[13] Emily Nagoski and Amelia Nagoski, *Burnout: The Secret to Unlocking the Stress Cycle* (New York: Ballantine Books, 2020).

[14] National Council of State Boards of Nursing, "NCSBN Research Projects Significant Nursing Workforce Shortages and Crisis," ncsbn.org, April 13, 2023, www.ncsbn.org/news/ncsbn-research-projects-significant-nursing-workforce-shortages-and-crisis.

[15] National Council of State Boards of Nursing, "NCSBN Research."

[16] I first wrote about how God welcomes our pain in the article "What to Do When Work Disappoints," Fuller De Pree Center, September 12, 2022, https://depree.org/what-to-do-when-work-disappoints. Used with permission.

2. FEELING LIKE AN EXILE

[1] These three options come from Albert O. Hirschman's *Exit, Voice, and Loyalty: Responses to Decline in Firms, Organizations, and States* (Cambridge, MA: Harvard University Press, 1970).

[2] Henri J. M. Nouwen, Donald P. McNeill, and Douglas A. Morrison, *Compassion: A Reflection on the Christian Life*, rev. ed. (New York: Doubleday, 2005), 70.

[3] Walter Wangerin Jr., *Mourning into Dancing* (Grand Rapids, MI: Zondervan, 1992), 91.

[4] Wangerin, *Mourning into Dancing*, 92.

[5] Brené Brown, *Atlas of the Heart: Mapping Meaningful Connection and the Language of Human Experience* (New York: Random House, 2021), 111.

[6] K.J. Ramsey, *This Too Shall Last: Finding Grace When Suffering Lingers* (Grand Rapids, MI: Zondervan, 2020), 22, Kindle.

[7] Nouwen, McNeill, and Morrison, *Compassion*, 70-71.

[8] Amos prophesied to the Northern Kingdom, "Jeroboam will die by the sword, And Israel will surely go into exile, Away from their native land" (Amos 7:11).

[9] Tokunboh Adeyemo, ed., *Africa Bible Commentary: A One-Volume Commentary Written by Seventy African Scholars*, rev. ed. (Grand Rapids, MI: Zondervan, 2010), 737.

[10] Adeyemo, *Africa Bible Commentary*, 737.

3. LEARNING TO SEE IN THE DARK

[1] These three options come from Albert O. Hirschman's *Exit, Voice, and Loyalty: Responses to Decline in Firms, Organizations, and States* (Cambridge, MA: Harvard University Press, 1970).

Henri J. M. Nouwen, Donald P. McNeill, and Douglas A. Morrison, *Compassion: A Reflection on the Christian Life*, rev. ed. (New York: Doubleday, 2005), 70-71.

[2]Parker J. Palmer, *Let Your Life Speak: Listening for the Voice of Vocation* (San Francisco: Jossey-Bass, 1999), 4-5.

[3]Walter A. Elwell, and Barry J. Beitzel, eds., "Exile," in *Baker Encyclopedia of the Bible* (Grand Rapids, MI: Baker, 1988), 732-36.

[4]Steven Garber, *Visions of Vocation: Common Grace for the Common Good* (Downers Grove, IL: InterVarsity Press, 2014), 18.

[5]Miroslav Volf, *Public Faith: How Followers of Christ Should Serve the Common Good* (Grand Rapids, MI: Brazos, 2011), xvi.

[6]Isaac Watts, "Joy to the World" (1719).

[7]Parker J. Palmer, "The Clearness Committee: A Communal Approach to Discernment," Center for Courage and Renewal, accessed January 27, 2024, https://couragerenewal.org/library/the-clearness-committee-a-communal-approach-to-discernment/.

[8]Arthur Bennett, ed., *The Valley of Vision: A Collection of Puritan Prayers and Devotions* (Edinburgh: Banner of Truth Trust, 1975), xxiv.

[9]Deidre Dukes, "Kemp Signs Georgia School Voucher Bill amid Controversy," Fox 5 Atlanta, April 23, 2024, www.fox5atlanta.com/news/kemp-signs-georgia-school-voucher-bill-amid-controversy.

4. SENSING A NEW CALLING

[1]Susan L. Maros, *Calling in Context: Social Location and Vocational Formation* (Downers Grove, IL: InterVarsity Press, 2022), 38.

[2]Steven Garber, *The Seamless Life: A Tapestry of Love and Learning, Worship and Work* (Downers Grove, IL: InterVarsity Press, 2020), 43.

[3]Bill Burnett and Dave Evans use the image of wayfinding in their book *Designing Your Life: How to Build a Well-Lived, Joyful Life* (New York: Knopf, 2016), but they focus primarily on paying attention to your life—your engagement and energy. I expand wayfinding to include paying attention to God, our community, and the world, in addition to ourselves.

[4]Sandy Ong, "What We Can Learn from the Ancient Art of Wayfinding," *BBC*, November 29, 2023, www.bbc.com/future/article/20231128-what-we-can-learn-from-the-ancient-art-of-wayfinding.

[5]Gordon T. Smith, *Courage and Calling: Embracing Your God-Given Potential*, rev. and expanded ed. (Downers Grove, IL: InterVarsity Press, 2011), 51.

[6]Brad Bell, "A Dislocated Heart: Nehemiah 1:1-4," sermon, The Well, September 4, 2009, https://thewellcommunity.org/podcasts/sermons/nehemiah-a-dislocated-heart.

[7]Frederick Buechner, *Wishful Thinking: A Seeker's ABC* (San Francisco: HarperOne, 1993), 95.

[8] Maros, *Calling in Context*, 48.

[9] Parts of this section on losing our sense of calling are adapted from my article "Lost: Three Reasons We Lose Our Sense of Calling," which first appeared on October 14, 2022, at depree.org, https://depree.org/lost-three-reasons-we-lose-our-sense-of-calling/, used with permission.

[10] This section has been adapted from my article "Found: How to Recover Our Sense of Calling," which first appeared on October 28, 2022, at depree.org, https://depree.org/found-how-to-recover-our-sense-of-calling/, used with permission.

5. STAYING ON TASK

[1] Gallup, "How Millennials Want to Work and Live," 2016, www.gallup.com/workplace/238073/millennials-work-live.aspx?thank-you-report-form=1.

[2] Joseph B Fuller, Manjari Raman, Eva Sage-Gavin, and Kristen Hines, "Hidden Workers: Untapped Talent," Harvard Business School Project on Managing the Future of Work and Accenture, September 2021, www.hbs.edu/managing-the-future-of-work/Documents/research/hiddenworkers09032021.pdf.

[3] Federal Trade Commission, "Protections Against Discrimination and Other Prohibited Practices," 2024, www.ftc.gov/policy-notices/no-fear-act/protections-against-discrimination.

[4] Patrick M. Kline, Evan K. Rose, and Christopher R. Walters, "Systemic Discrimination Among Large U.S. Employers," National Bureau of Economic Research, May 2022, www.nber.org/system/files/working_papers/w29053/w29053.pdf.

[5] LeanIn.Org and McKinsey & Company, "Women in the Workplace Study: The State of Women in Corporate America," Lean In, 2023, https://leanin.org/women-in-the-workplace#.

[6] Emerson Dameron and Christine Clark, "When Job Seekers Are 'Overqualified,' Gender Bias May Come into Play," *UC San Diego Today* (blog), January 31, 2022, https://today.ucsd.edu/story/when-job-seekers-are-overqualified-gender-bias-may-come-into-play.

6. MAKING SENSE OF IT ALL

[1] Crystal L. Park, "Making Sense of the Meaning Literature: An Integrative Review of Meaning Making and Its Effects on Adjustment to Stressful Life Events," *Psychological Bulletin* 136, no. 2 (2010): 257-301.

[2]Jack Mezirow, "Learning to Think like an Adult: Core Concepts of Transformation Theory," in *The Handbook of Transformative Learning: Theory, Research, and Practice*, ed. Edward W. Taylor and Patricia Cranton and Associates (San Francisco: Jossey-Bass, 2012), 73-95.

[3]Jane E. Dutton and Amy Wrzesniewski, "What Job Crafting Looks Like," *Harvard Business Review*, March 12, 2020, https://hbr.org/2020/03/what-job-crafting-looks-like.

[4]Bryan J. Dik and Ryan D. Duffy, *Make Your Job a Calling: How the Psychology of Vocation Can Change Our Life at Work* (West Conshohocken, PA: Templeton Press, 2012), 37.

[5]Dik and Duffy, *Make Your Job a Calling*, 11.

[6]Dik and Duffy, *Make Your Job a Calling*, 89.

[7]Arthur C. Brooks, "The Only Career Advice You'll Ever Need," *The Atlantic*, May 18, 2023, www.theatlantic.com/ideas/archive/2023/05/career-advice-happiness-know-thyself/674087/.

[8]Susan L. Maros, *Calling in Context: Social Location and Vocational Formation* (Downers Grove, IL: InterVarsity Press, 2022), 43.

[9]Tish Harrison Warren, *Prayer in the Night: For Those Who Work or Watch or Weep* (Downers Grove, IL: InterVarsity Press, 2021), 65.

[10]Andy Crouch, *Culture Making: Recovering Our Creative Calling* (Downers Grove, IL: InterVarsity Press, 2008), 23.

7. WORKING IN A BATTLE ZONE

[1]S. Sleek, "Toxic Workplaces Leave Employees Sick, Scared, and Looking for an Exit. How to Combat Unhealthy Conditions," *American Psychological Association*, July 13, 2023, www.apa.org/topics/healthy-workplaces/toxic-workplace.

[2]D. Sull, C. Sull, and B. Zweig, "Toxic Culture Is Driving the Great Resignation," *MIT Sloan Management Review*, January 11, 2022, https://sloanreview.mit.edu/article/toxic-culture-is-driving-the-great-resignation/.

[3]Donald Sull, Charles Sull, William Cipolli, and Ciao Brighenti, "Why Every Leader Needs to Worry About Toxic Culture," *MIT Sloan Management Review*, March 16, 2022, https://sloanreview.mit.edu/article/why-every-leader-needs-to-worry-about-toxic-culture/.

[4]Nupanga Weanzana, "Nehemiah," in *Africa Bible Commentary: A One-Volume Commentary Written by Seventy African Scholars*, rev. ed., ed. Tokunboh Adeyemo (Grand Rapids, MI: Zondervan, 2010), 543-88, 545. See also L. S. Tiemeyer, "Sanballat," in *Dictionary of the Old Testament: Historical*

Books, ed. Bill T. Arnold and H. G. M. Williamson (Downers Grove, IL: IVP Academic, 2005), 877-80.

⁵M. Priesemuth, "Time's Up for Toxic Workplaces," *Harvard Business Review*, June 19, 2020, https://hbr.org/2020/06/times-up-for-toxic-workplaces.

⁶Vicki Webster, Paula Brough, and Kathleen Daly, "Fight, Flight, or Freeze: Common Responses for Follower Coping with Toxic Leadership," *Stress and Health* 32 (2016): 346-54.

⁷Albert O. Hirschman, *Exit, Voice, and Loyalty: Responses to Decline in Firms, Organizations, and States* (Cambridge, MA: Harvard University Press, 1970).

⁸Hirschman, *Exit, Voice, and Loyalty*, 38.

⁹Brent A. Strawn, "Imprecation," in *Dictionary of the Old Testament: Wisdom, Poetry & Writings*, ed. Tremper Longman III and Peter Enns (Downers Grove, IL: IVP Academic, 2008), 317.

¹⁰Tish Harrison Warren, "Go Ahead. Pray for Putin's Demise," *Christianity Today*, March 8, 2022, www.christianitytoday.com/ct/2022/march-web-only/prayer-ukraine-russia-putin-imprecatory-psalms.html.

¹¹Strawn, "Imprecation," 318.

¹²U.S. Bureau of Labor Statistics, "Workplace Violence: Homicides and Nonfatal Intentional Injuries by Another Person in 2020," *TED: The Economics Daily* (blog), November 21, 2022, www.bls.gov/opub/ted/2022/workplace-violence-homicides-and-nonfatal-intentional-injuries-by-another-person-in-2020.htm.

¹³Klyne Snodgrass, *Ephesians*, NIV Application Commentary (Grand Rapids, MI: Zondervan, 1996), 355.

¹⁴Elaine Howard Ecklund, Brenton Kalinowski, and Denise Daniels, "Thinking About Work as a Calling Can Be Meaningful, but There Can Be Unexpected Downsides as Well," *The Conversation* (blog), January 25, 2024, https://theconversation.com/thinking-about-work-as-a-calling-can-be-meaningful-but-there-can-be-unexpected-downsides-as-well-216970.

¹⁵Stuart J. Bunderson and Jeffrey A. Thompson, "The Call of the Wild: Zookeepers, Callings, and the Double-Edged Sword of Deeply Meaningful Work," *Administrative Science Quarterly* 54, no. 1 (2009): 32-57.

¹⁶K.J. Ramsey, *The Lord Is My Courage* (Grand Rapids, MI: Zondervan Reflective, 2022), 169.

¹⁷Ramsey, *Lord Is My Courage*, 171.

¹⁸Ramsey, *Lord Is My Courage*, 173.

8. BEING EXPLOITED AND OPPRESSED

[1] Statista Research Department, "Annual Net Sales Revenue of Amazon from 2004 to 2022," August 29, 2023, www.statista.com/statistics/266282/annual-net-revenue-of-amazoncom/.

[2] Jay Greene, "Amazon's Employee Surveillance Fuels Unionization Efforts: 'It's Not Prison, It's Work,'" *The Washington Post*, December 2, 2021, www.washingtonpost.com/technology/2021/12/02/amazon-workplace-monitoring-unions/.

[3] Irene Tung and Alyssa Tufano, "Amazon Workers Are Injured Almost Twice as Often as Other Warehouse Workers in Massachusetts," *National Employment Law Project* (blog), March 13, 2023, www.nelp.org/publication/amazon-workers-are-injured-almost-twice-as-often-as-other-warehouse-workers-in-massachusetts/.

[4] U.S. Department of Labor, "U.S. Department of Labor Finds Amazon Exposed Workers to Unsafe Conditions, Ergonomic Hazards at Three More Warehouses in Colorado, Idaho, New York," February 1, 2023, www.dol.gov/newsroom/releases/osha/osha20230201-0.

[5] U.S. Department of Labor, "The Essential Workers of the Coronavirus Pandemic," Hall of Honor Inductees, 2022, www.dol.gov/general/aboutdol/hallofhonor/2022-essential-workers.

[6] Alex Russell, "Low-Wage Workers Are Often Trapped, Unable to Advance," UC Davis Department of Sociology, 2024, https://sociology.ucdavis.edu/research/research-spotlight/faculty-research-spotlight/low-wage-workers-are-often-trapped-unable-to-advance-1.

[7] Global Labor Justice, "Precarious Work," *Issues* (blog), 2024, https://laborrights.org/issues/precarious-work.

[8] International Labour Organization and Canadian Autoworkers, "Precarious Work," August 1, 2011, www.ilo.org/resource/canadian-autoworkers-precarious-work.

[9] International Labour Organization and Canadian Autoworkers, "Precarious Work."

[10] Lori Botterman, "Study Reveals Precarious Employment on the Rise Long before COVID-19," *UIC Today* (blog), January 27, 2021, https://today.uic.edu/study-reveals-precarious-employment-on-the-rise-long-before-covid-19/.

[11] Botterman, "Study Reveals Precarious Employment."

[12] Emma Ross, "Fast Fashion Getting Faster: A Look at the Unethical Labor Practices Sustaining a Growing Industry," *GW Law International Law and*

Policy Brief (blog), October 28, 2021, https://studentbriefs.law.gwu.edu/ilpb/2021/10/28/fast-fashion-getting-faster-a-look-at-the-unethical-labor-practices-sustaining-a-growing-industry/.

[13] Ross, "Fast Fashion."

[14] Ross, "Fast Fashion."

[15] Charlie Campbell, "Dying for Some New Clothes: Bangladesh's Rana Plaza Tragedy," *Time*, April 26, 2013, https://world.time.com/2013/04/26/dying-for-some-new-clothes-the-tragedy-of-rana-plaza/.

[16] Ruben Rosalez, "The Exploitation of Garment Workers: Threading the Needle on Fast Fashion," United States Department of Labor Blog, March 21, 2023, https://blog.dol.gov/2023/03/21/the-exploitation-of-garment-workers-threading-the-needle-on-fast-fashion.

[17] National Council for Occupational Safety and Health (National COSH), "Dirty Dozen 2023," April 2023, https://nationalcosh.org/Dirty-Dozen-2023.

[18] International Labour Organization, Walk Free, and International Organization for Migration, "Global Estimates of Modern Slavery: Forced Labour and Forced Marriage," ilo.org, September 19, 2022, www.walkfree.org/reports/global-estimates-of-modern-slavery-2022/.pdf, 14.

[19] International Labour Organization et al., "Global Estimates," 17.

[20] Department of Homeland Security, "What Is Forced Labor?" Blue Campaign, 2024, www.dhs.gov/blue-campaign/forced-labor.

[21] Lautaro Grinspan, "Investigators Uncovered 'Modern-Day Slavery' on Georgia Farms. What's Next for Victims?" *The Atlanta Journal-Constitution*, January 5, 2022, www.ajc.com/news/georgia-news/investigators-uncovered-modern-day-slavery-on-georgia-farms-whats-next-for-victims/RIOCY5JIWRHCVDY5USYAILEF44/#.

[22] Lautaro Grinspan, "'This Has Been Happening for a Long Time': Modern-Day Slavery Uncovered in South Georgia," *The Atlanta Journal-Constitution*, December 3, 2021, www.ajc.com/news/this-has-been-happening-for-a-long-time-modern-day-slavery-uncovered-in-ga/SHBHTDDTTBG3BCPSVCB3GQ66BQ/#.

[23] International Labour Organization et al., "Global Estimates," 43. Italics original.

[24] Josh Bivens, "CEO Pay Slightly Declined in 2022," *Economic Policy Institute* (blog), September 21, 2023, www.epi.org/publication/ceo-pay-in-2022/.

[25] Max De Pree, *Leadership Is an Art*, repr. ed. (New York: Crown, 2004), 65.

[26] De Pree, *Leadership Is an Art*, 98.

27. Kamala D. Harris, "The California Transparency in Supply Chains Act: A Resource Guide," California Department of Justice, 2015, https://oag.ca.gov/sites/all/files/agweb/pdfs/sb657/resource-guide.pdf.

28. State of California Department of Justice, "The California Transparency in Supply Chains Act," 2024, https://oag.ca.gov/SB657.

29. Elaine Wood, Brad Dragoon, Emily Butler, Dave Curran, and Madhuri Pavamani, "Risk in the Supply Chain: Proposed Laws Seek Unprecedented Transparency," *Business Law Today* (blog), July 12, 2022, https://businesslawtoday.org/2022/07/risk-supply-chain-proposed-laws-seek-unprecedented-transparency-fashion-sustainability-act/.

9. REALIZING IT'S ME

1. Tony Schwartz and Eric Severson, "Why We Glorify Overwork and Refuse to Rest," *Harvard Business Review*, August 28, 2023, https://hbr.org/2023/08/why-we-glorify-overwork-and-refuse-to-rest.

2. Mark Throntveit, *Ezra-Nehemiah*, Interpretation (Louisville: Westminster John Knox Press, 1992), 97.

3. Brené Brown, *Daring Greatly: How the Courage to Be Vulnerable Transforms the Way We Live, Love, Parent, and Lead* (New York: Avery, 2012), 37.

4. Bryan J. Dik and Ryan D. Duffy, *Make Your Job a Calling: How the Psychology of Vocation Can Change Our Life at Work* (West Conshohocken, PA: Templeton Press, 2012), 114.

10. REMEMBERING TO HOPE

1. National Conference on State Legislatures, "At-Will Employment—Overview," nscl.org, April 15, 2008, www.ncsl.org/labor-and-employment/at-will-employment-overview; The Brothers Grimm, "The Fairytale of Hansel and Gretel," trans. Joyce Crick, *The Guardian*, October 10, 2009, www.theguardian.com/books/2009/oct/10/fairytales-hansel-gretel.

2. Curt Thompson, *Anatomy of the Soul: Surprising Connections between Neuroscience and Spiritual Practices That Can Transform Your Life and Relationships* (Carol Stream, IL: Tyndale Refresh, 2010), 72.

3. Sally Lloyd-Jones, *The Jesus Storybook Bible* (Grand Rapids, MI: Zondervan, 2007), 36.

4. Psychologist Martin Seligman developed the three good things exercise. Learn more at https://ggia.berkeley.edu/practice/three-good-things.

Like this book?
Scan the code to discover more content like this!

Get on IVP's email list to receive special offers, exclusive book news, and thoughtful content from your favorite authors on topics you care about.

IVPRESS.COM/BOOK-QR